Interiors
in Red

ROCKPORT PUBLISHERS
GLOUCESTER, MASSACHUSETTS

First published in the United States of America by:
Rockport Publishers, Inc.
33 Commercial Street
Gloucester, Massachusetts 01930-5089
Telephone: (978) 282-9590
Facsimile: (978) 283-2742

Distributed to the book trade and art trade in the United States by:
North Light Books, an imprint of
F & W Publications
1507 Dana Avenue
Cincinnati, Ohio 45207
Telephone: (800) 289-0963

Other Distribution by:
Rockport Publishers, Inc.
Gloucester, Massachusetts 01930-5089

ISBN 1-56496-442-6

10 9 8 7 6 5 4 3 2 1

Designer: Karen Rappaport
Cover Image: Interior Design Sandra Nunnerly Inc.
          See page 76

Printed in Hong Kong by Midas Printing Limited.

For more beautiful work by the designers and photographers featured in this collection, please see:

Showcase of Interior Design: Eastern Edition 1
Showcase of Interior Design: Eastern Edition 2
Showcase of Interior Design: Eastern Edition 3
Showcase of Interior Design: Midwest Edition 1
Showcase of Interior Design: Midwest Edition 2
Showcase of Interior Design: Pacific Edition 1
Showcase of Interior Design: Pacific Edition 2
Showcase of Interior Design: Southern Edition 1
Showcase of Interior Design: Southern Edition 2
Colors for Living: Bedrooms by Carol Meredith
Colors for Living: Living Rooms by Jennie Pugh
Eclectic Style in Interior Design by Carol Meredith

Passion, heat, romance: the vibrancy of red is indisputable. A room saturated in red will be ablaze with color and demand attention. Even red accents will become the focal point of an otherwise neutral room. Red decorations will bring a touch of warmth and vitality to a room of cool colors. In combination with blue and yellow, red will add a sense of playfulness and energy. Red brings out the richness of color in a cherry table, and complements the rich tones of mahogany. The placement of color is as important as the choice of red itself: red in a living room will bring warmth and vitality, red in an entrance will be inviting, red in the dining room will add a regal atmosphere, and red in a bedroom will add drama and richness. Each person's emotional response to a color is entirely subjective. With all the spectrum to choose from, it is near impossible not to find the perfect red for any room of your home.

(right and below) INTERIOR DESIGN
Carl Steele Associates, Inc.

(opposite page) INTERIOR DESIGN
M. L. Slovack Design, Inc.

(below) INTERIOR DESIGN
Elaine Bass Interiors

(above) Facilitated client's move from a large home to
a high-rise condominium by adapting client's furniture,
accessories and antiques to their new home.

INTERIOR DESIGN
Arlis Ede Interiors, Inc.

(above) Against the backdrop of a rich red wall,
primitive masks crown this lofty study space and look
down upon furnishings from centuries after their time.

INTERIOR DESIGN
John Robert Wiltgen Design

Photo: Jim Hedrich, Hedrich Blessing

(above) The feeling of the ski
house is more European than
southwestern; the large Louis
XIV armoire makes a very
strong statement in the big
living room.

INTERIOR DESIGN

David Webster & Associates

(right) INTERIOR DESIGN

Kathleen Buoymaster, Inc.

Photo: Edward Gohlich

(left) A leather sofa, marble floor and vibrant painting highlight this beautifully appointed sitting area.

INTERIOR DESIGN
Kuckly Associates, Inc.

(left, below) A sunny, carefree room offers plenty of comfort, while serving as a showcase for a collection of pre-Columbian art.

INTERIOR DESIGN
Jennifer Garrigues, Inc.

(below) Refurbishment helped brighten and update St. Louis Mayor Freeman R. Bosley Jr.'s turn-of-the-century office in City Hall.

INTERIOR DESIGN
Carrie Brockman's Design Group

(above) In a room without architectural integrity, simple early twentieth-century details, the clients' collection of Cubist paintings, and neoclassical furniture were combined to create a layered and welcoming environment.

INTERIOR DESIGN
Brian J. McCarthy, Inc.

(left) Part of a master suite, this octagonal sitting room features a 20-foot turreted ceiling and French doors that open onto balconies overlooking a lake. French furnishings and sumptuous fabrics add to the aura of elegance.

INTERIOR DESIGN

Diane Wendell Interior Design

(above) New construction was given an old world feel by richly glazing walls, and using heavy textured fabrics in this den and library—private residence, Mr. and Mrs. Don Ware, Abbotsford, Nashville, Tennessee.

INTERIOR DESIGN

G. S. Hinsen Company

(right) Introducing a bold, modern fabric quickens the pulse of any room.

INTERIOR DESIGN
Bierly-Drake Associates

Photo: Sam Gray

(below) Family photos and mementos help personalize the quiet sitting room retreat off the master bedroom.

INTERIOR DESIGN
Meadowbank Designs, Inc.

(opposite page) Against a brilliant red wall, the poster becomes the room's focal point. Intense color draws the viewer's eye, and the black frame and white border intensify the effect.

INTERIOR DESIGN
Lovick Design

Photo: Art Grey

(above) Antiques, accessories, lighting, carpet, wallpaper, and reproduction settee—all with an "exotic" oriental feeling—create layers of pattern on pattern, complementing every surface in this sitting room.

INTERIOR DESIGN
Stingray Hornsby Interiors

(right) INTERIOR DESIGN
Dorothy H. Travis Interiors, Inc.

(right) A coffee table stained with rich Moroccan henna holds two rare Spanish colonial santos.

INTERIOR DESIGN

David Dalton Associates

(below) A cozy library features a bold mix of patterns and textures.

INTERIOR DESIGN

Diane Alpern Kovacs Interior Design, Inc.

(opposite page) Incorporating one or two strong design elements creates focus in rooms teeming with objects and collectibles. In the parlor, the most powerful elements are red walls and one large piece of art.

INTERIOR DESIGN

Claude Guidi

Photo: Steve Vierra

24

(below) Deep cherry walls with white moldings and a custom designed bookcase/dry bar made a bold statement softened by yellow florals, Persian rugs, and exquisite accessories. This room was designed to stand up to the test of time and eight grandchildren.

INTERIOR DESIGN
Lynn Robinson Interiors

(right) The entertainment center and tables designed by Bobbi Packer Designs are in the client's favorite colors. The space functions as the family's gathering room.

INTERIOR DESIGN
Bobbi Packer Designs

(below) The oversize living room of this residence has as its focus the magnificent formal gardens beyond the large bay window.

INTERIOR DESIGN
Trilogy

(above) INTERIOR DESIGN

Barbara Lazarus

(right) INTERIOR DESIGN

Clifford Stiles McAlpin Interiors, Inc.

(above) INTERIOR DESIGN

Claude Guidi

Photo: Steve Vierra

(above) The owner's love of animals
is reflected in a range of details,
from elephants parading across the
valance to the ceramic pieces that
grace tabletops and bookshelves.

INTERIOR DESIGN
Fran Murphy & Associates

The upholstered walls of the room add an extra warmth to this niche, which contains a drop arm sofa and a chinoise coffee table set with antique decanters and glasses.

INTERIOR DESIGN

Antine Associates

The warmth of the room is achieved by using a mixture of elegant fabrics, fine antiques and collectables, and wonderfully comfortable upholstery. The chinoise secretary is seventeenth century, the bull's eye mirror eighteenth century, and the rug later nineteenth century. The walls are upholstered in Scottish wool woven in a Russian pattern.

INTERIOR DESIGN

Antine Associates

(above) INTERIOR DESIGN

Judy McMurray

Photo: Steve Vierra

(above) Rich colored walls
and furnishings combined with
the strong natural light provide
a cozy haven for reading,
watching television, or enjoying
the company of friends and
relatives.

INTERIOR DESIGN
Sue Wenk Interior Design Inc.

(below) Warm, comfortable setting combines French and
English antiques with collections
of Meissen, Derby and Imari.

INTERIOR DESIGN
Rodgers Menzies Interior Design

(above) A crisp country English setting is created in this historic Pennsylvania farmhouse. Antiques subtly fill the room, and color and pattern mix like old friends.

INTERIOR DESIGN

Meadowbank Designs, Inc.

(right) INTERIOR DESIGN

Arlene Semel & Associates, Inc.

(below) To make this formal living room more approachable while still imparting an air of elegance, the warm tones of the Oushak rug are used throughout, while a collection of interesting and unusual accessories punctuates the seating areas.

INTERIOR DESIGN

C. Weaks Interiors, Inc.

(left) An intimate fireplace area combines wood and stone with warm, jewel-toned colorations in the antique area rug and occasional seating.

INTERIOR DESIGN
Ron Hefler

(below) Room With a View— all upholstery custom designed and built, eclectic mixture of antiques and styles

INTERIOR DESIGN
Chambers Interiors and Associates, Inc.

(left) This library, formerly a garage, serves as the informal gathering place for a large family.

INTERIOR DESIGN

Trilogy

(above) A sofa from Baker Furniture and an antique Irish Chippendale tea table are just two of the highlights in this living room. The painting above the mantel—"Going Home"—is 150 years old.

INTERIOR DESIGN

Myrl Talkington Designs

(above) Rich colors, exquisite furnishings and an abundance of architectural details work together to create the ultimate in refined living. Note the tromp l'oeil "alcoves" on the right.

INTERIOR DESIGN

Gernard Design Group

(left) An intricately orchestrated palette and elaborate detailing conspired with English, French and Italian antiques to create a rich eclectic interior of distinct personality.

INTERIOR DESIGN

Eberlein Design Consultants Ltd.

(below) Custom designed floral rug offers foundation for fresh, vibrant color scheme; warms a large room overlooking pool and lake.

INTERIOR DESIGN

Rodgers Menzies Interior Design

(right) Capitalizing on an already dark room, the deep green walls create a serene setting for a smallish living room and present the perfect backdrop for "Hairdresser," a 1948 painting by Russian-born Simka Simkhovitch.

(below right) "Cochise" the howling coyote sets the tone for this whimsy filled proch, a favorite summertime retreat.

INTERIOR DESIGN
Busch and Associates

(above) INTERIOR DESIGN

Kuhl Design Associates, Inc.

(below) A view of a living room with red walls and white ground chintz to emphasize the whimsical architectural details of this Victorian house.

INTERIOR DESIGN

Tonin MacCallum ASID Inc.

(above) A country library in an American pre-Revolutionary house has been created in an eclectic manner. A traditional linen floral fabric and needlepoint rug have been combined with a mirrored wall and Chinese lacquered coffee table.

INTERIOR DESIGN
Scott Salvator, Inc.

(above) Antique French furnishings collected
by the owners grace this new town house.

INTERIOR DESIGN

Clifford Stiles McAlpin Interiors, Inc.

(right) INTERIOR DESIGN

M.L. Slovack Design, Inc.

(above) A Gothic revival sitting room is born by vaulting a previously flat ceiling and ading cabinetry and moldings.

INTERIOR DESIGN
Henry Johnstone & Co.

(above) A heightened sense of
formality is accomplished with
heavily festooned windows,
damask wallcovering, silk upholstery and elegant accessories.

INTERIOR DESIGN
John Henry Sherman, Jr. Interiors

(right) INTERIOR DESIGN
Akins and Aylesworth

(right) INTERIOR DESIGN

Susan Kroeger, Ltd.

(below) INTERIOR DESIGN

J. Westerfield Antiques & Interiors, Inc.

(above) Dramatic use of colorful fluid
forms makes this "L"-shaped family
room an exciting place to expand
one's horizons.

INTERIOR DESIGN

Pedlar's Village Interior Design

(above) An Old World map on faux parchment
was commissioned for the ceiling of this library.
The furniture, artwork, antique Persian rug and
leather wall panels create a rich, worldly effect.

INTERIOR DESIGN

Suzanne Stacey McCallen / G. S. Hinsen Compoany

(above) A bronze "Big Bird" and an intriguing sculpture on the coffee table are among the many special collectibles that give this apartment a flavor all its own.

INTERIOR DESIGN
S & B Interiors, Inc.

(lef) INTERIOR DESIGN
Kuhl Design Associates, Inc.

(right) INTERIOR DESIGN
Joan Halperin/Interior Design

(below) Many cherished possessions fit comfortably into this vibrantly colorful keeping room.

INTERIOR DESIGN
Rodgers Menzies Interior Design

(above) A crisp country English setting
is created in this historic Pennsylvania
farmhouse. Antiques subtly fill the
room, and color and pattern mix
like old friends.

INTERIOR DESIGN
Meadowbank Designs, Inc.

(above) INTERIOR DESIGN

Joan Spiro Interiors

(right) Turnberry Isle Beauty Salon

INTERIOR DESIGN

JoyCe Stolberg Interiors, Inc.

(right) Louis, Boston

INTERIOR DESIGN

Stedila Design, Inc.

(right) The dining room in this historical house, built circa 1750 and later relocated to an oceanfront site, possesses a wonderful Normandy feel. An oil portrait of Mrs. Baker —the original owner of the house—presides over the long room at last, after residing in the attic for some time. The color scheme is now brighter, bridging the past to the present.

INTERIOR DESIGN

Alexis E. Benne Interiors

(below right) A mix of antiue chairs with Fortuny upholstery and modern architecture creates a contemporary and romantic setting in this restaurant.

INTERIOR DESIGN

L.B.D.A. Design Associates, Inc.

(opposite page) Modern art, new furniture, and the unexpected red color of the mantel add personal flair to a house with traditional architecture.

INTERIOR DESIGN

Ida Goldstein

Photo: Steve Vierra

(above) The elements used in this small, square dining room were selected to make maximum use of space while highlighting the sense of intimacy. Replacing the traditional rectangular table and long sideboard with a round table and pair of demilune cabinets allows for ease of movement without sacrificing seating or storage.

INTERIOR DESIGN

C. Weaks Interiors, Inc.

(right) INTERIOR DESIGN

J. Dayvault & Associates

(below right) Here, sleek design is accented with a Southwestern flair. The older cabinets feature an autumn red heirloom finish. Reflections of light bounce from the absolute black granite tile countertops. Eagle, Colorado.

INTERIOR DESIGN

Thurston Kitchen & Bath

(above) INTERIOR DESIGN

Cricket Interiors

(below) This eclectic living room works in large part because of its unifying color scheme of red, brown, gold, and soft yellow.

INTERIOR DESIGN
Samuel Botero Associates

Photo: Phillip H. Ennis

(right) Permanent murals set the color palette, individual dining tables counterbalance formality.

INTERIOR DESIGN
Klingmans of Grand Rapids

(left) Antique Irish Chippendale chairs, a Serapi
rug, and a period mahogany sheraton server work
together to create a breathtaking effect.

INTERIOR DESIGN
Myrl Talkington Designs

(below) Hand-painted glazed walls, silk
lined damask draped windows and a 19th
century French chandelier set the stage for
entertaining meals.

INTERIOR DESIGN
Julie Lanterman Interior Designs

(*above*) Custom valances with an awning
effect evoke thoughts of dining alfresco, while
the furnishings set the mood for sumptuously
comfortable dining.

INTERIOR DESIGN
Samantha Cole

(left) Iron, pine, mahogany and natural fibers contribute to the warmth and coziness of a Boca Raton, Florida, breakfast room.

(below) Rich upholstery fabrics provide a subtle contrast to a bare wood floor.

INTERIOR DESIGN

Interior Designs by Daphne Weiss, Inc.

(above) Neoclassic in reference, the custom dining table has a top of figured mahogany with gilt detailing on the pedestals and feet. A collection of blanc de chine porcelain is indirectly lit within the display vitrine, which is lacquered the same cherry as the walls.

INTERIOR DESIGN
Sandra Nunnerley Inc.

(right) A George II console and an old Venetian painting (attributed to Jacabo Bassano) introduce a generous helping of dining elegance.

INTERIOR DESIGN
Cesar Lucian Scaff, Inc.

(above) INTERIOR DESIGN

Cricket Interiors

(above) INTERIOR DESIGN
James R. Irving, ASID

(left) The mixing of an antique
hutch and accessories with a
reproduction dining table and
chairs creates a cozy area
for casual or formal dining.

INTERIOR DESIGN

J. Powell & Associates, Inc.

(above) Luxurious, durable ultra
suede covers the seating pieces
in the living room, while silk
fabric is used in the dining area.

INTERIOR DESIGN
S & B Interiors, Inc.

(right) Lavish dinner parties
originate from this spectacular
backdrop.

INTERIOR DESIGN
Julie Lanterman Interior Designs

(left) A custom designed, Gothic-style mirror hangs above an early 18th century chest of drawers. Complementing the architecture is a wainscot inscribed with a trefoil pattern.

INTERIOR DESIGN

Henry Johnstone & Co.

(above) A cozy dining room brings together antique treasures and provides a dramatic setting for the riding portrait of a relative. The colors in the custom carpet further enhance this warm and intimate dining space.

INTERIOR DESIGN

Meadowbank Designs Inc.

(right) 1855 French scenic paper, a fine French chandelier above antique furnishings and red damask walls. Architecture by Stephen Kubenka, AIA.

INTERIOR DESIGN

Nicholson Interiors

(right) Collections tell a story about the people who live with them. In this historic New England home, heirlooms passed through generations speak of a venerable past, from family portraits to a wooden water bucket, now hanging from the ceiling, used to douse fires by an eighteenth century relative. Pedigree makes way for playfulness on the stair-way, where the owner's collection of antique miniature chests whimsically climb the stairs.

Photo: Eric Roth

(above) INTERIOR DESIGN

In-Site Design Group Inc.

(above) The custom desk is
designed to fit seamlessly into
the overall environment.

INTERIOR DESIGN
V-3 Design

(above) Tiles from the 1920s inspired the decorations
of this guest bath.

INTERIOR DESIGN
Henry Johnstone & Co.

(right) Photo: Steve Vierra

Two elements balance this room against the dramatic saturated red wall: The abundance of solid white gives off light, and the horizontal lines of the shoji screens increase the sense of spaciousness.

Photo: Steve Vierra

(above) Curved walls and dramatic window treatments help this spacious master bedroom seem almost enveloping. The massive French rope-twist poster bed reproduction is beautifully at home with the 18th century French walnut armoire.

INTERIOR DESIGN

Meadowbank Designs, Inc.

(above) The passion of red and the opulence
of gold harmonize in this master bedroom.

INTERIOR DESIGN

Brito Interior Design, Inc.

(above) INTERIOR DESIGN

Barbara Lazarus

Akins & Aylesworth, Ltd.
26 E. First Street
Hinsdale, IL 60521
630/325.3355
Fax: 630/325.3315

Alexis E. Benné Interiors
100 Riverside Drive
New York, NY 10024
212/580.8118
Fax: 212/769.0809

Antine Associates
1028 Arcadian Way
Fort Lee, NJ 07024
201/224.0315
Fax: 201/224.5963

Arlene Semel & Associates, Inc.
445 N. Franklin
Chicago, IL 60610
312/644.1480
Fax: 312/644.8157
e-mail: asasemel@aol.com

Arlis Ede Interiors, Inc.
3520 Fairmount
Dallas, TX 75219
214/521.1302
Fax: 214/559.4729

Barbara Lazarus
10 Fones Alley
Providence, RI 02906
401/521.8910
Fax: 401/438.8809

Bobbi Packer Designs
126 Edgecliffe Drive
Highland Park, IL 60035
847/432.0407
Fax: 847/432.0490

Brian J. McCarthy, Inc.
1414 Avenue of the Americas
Suite 404
New York, NY 10019
212/308.7600
Fax: 212/308.4242

Bierly-Drake Associates, Inc.
17 Arlington Street
Boston, MA 02116

Brito Interiors
1000 Quayside Terrace, #412
Miami, FL 33138
305/895/8539
Fax: 305/893.1962

Brown's Interiors, Inc.
1115 Kenilworth Avenue
Charlotte, NC 28204
704/375.2248
Fax: 704/334.0982

Busch and Associates
1615 N. Mohawk
Chicago, IL 60614
312/649.9106
Fax: 312/649.9106

Carl Steele Associates
1606 Pine Street
Philadelphia, PA 19103
215/546.5530
Fax: 215/546.1571

Carrie Brockman's Design Group
322 North Meramac
Clayton, OH 63105
314/726.6333
Fax: 314/721.0778

Cassina USA
200 McKay Road
Huntington Station, NY 11746

Cesar Lucian Scaff
9 Nantucket Court
Beechwood, OH 44122
216/831.2033
Fax: 216/360.0632

Chambers Interiors and
Associates, Inc.
2719 Laclede, Suite B
Dallas, TX 75204
214/871.9222
Fax: 214/871.0644

Claude Guidi
411 East 57th Street
New York, NY 10022

Clifford Stiles McAlpin
Interiors, Inc.
900 East Moreno Street
Pensacola, FL 32503
850/438.8345
Fax: 850/434.8315

Cricket Interiors
2505 Arlington Road
Cleveland Heights, OH 44118
216/321.5087
Fax: 216/321.9035
e-mail: helldeg@aol.com

C. Weaks Interiors, Inc.
3391 Habersham Road
Atlanta, GA 30305
404/233.6040
Fax: 404/233.6043

Daphne Weiss, Inc.
PO Box 7005
Boca Raton, FL 33431
561/392.6301
Fax: 561/395.4409
e-mail: dweiss4@ibm.net

David Dalton Associates
8687 Melrose Ave. Suite G290
Los Angeles, CA 90069
310/289.6010
Fax: 310/289.6011

David Webster & Associates
254 W. 25th Street
New York, NY 10001
212/924.8932
Fax: 212/477.3934

Diane Alpern Kovacs,
Interior Design Inc.
4 Main Street
Roslyn, NY 11576
516/625.0703
Fax: 516/625.8441
e-mail: cottagered@aol.com

Diane Wendell Interior Design
1121 Warren Avenue
Downers Grove, IL 60515
630/852.0235
Fax: 630/988.8341

Dorothy H. Travis Interiors, Inc.
12 Kings Circle, NE
Atlanta, GA
404/233.7210
Fax: 404/233.7260

Eberlein Design Consultants, Ltd.
1809 Walnut Street, Suite 410
Philadelphia, PA 19103
215/405.0400
Fax: 215/405.0588

Elaine Bass Interiors
11 Rutland Road
Great Neck, NY 11020
516/482.6834
Fax: 516/482.7138

Ellen Sosnow Interiors
850 Park Avenue
New York, NY 10021
212/744.0214
Fax: 212/772.3443

Fran Murphy & Associates
71 E. Allendale Road
Saddle River, NJ 07458
201/934.6029
Fax: 201/934.5597
e-mail: enm2@worldnet.att.net

Gerhard Design Group
7630 El Camino Real
Rancho La Costa, CA 92009
760/436.0181
Fax: 760/435.7945

G. S. Hinsen Co.
2133 Bandywood
Nashville, TN 37215
615/383.6440
Fax: 615/269.5130

Harte-Brownlee & Associates, Inc.
1691 Westcliff Drive
Newport Beach, CA 92660
714/548.9530
Fax: 714/548.9528

Henry Johnstone & Co.
95 San Miguel Road
Pasadena, CA 91105
818/716.7624
Fax: 818/716.0017

Ida Goldstein
16 Munnings Drive
Sudbury, MA 01776

In-Site Design Group Inc.
3551 S. Monaco Parkway
Denver, CO 80237
303/691.9000
Fax: 303/757.6475

James R. Irving, ASID
13901 Shaker Blvd.
Cleveland, OH 44120
216/283.1991

J. Dayvault & Associates
78 Peachtree Circle
Atlanta, GA 30309
404/873.1873
Fax: 404/873.4271
e-mail: jday@aol.com

Jennifer Garrigues, Inc.
308 Peruvian Avenue
Palm Beach, FL 33480
561/659.7085
Fax: 561/659.7090

Joan Halperin/Interior Design
401 East 80th Street
New York, NY 10021
212/288.8636
Fax: 212/472.3743

Joan Spiro Interiors
PO box 1170 OVS
Great Neck, NY 11023
516/829.9087
Fax: 516/829.1578

John Henry Sherman Jr. Interiors
9615 Thomas Drive
Panama City, FL 32407
850/233.0413
Fax: 850/230.9035

John Robert Wiltgen Design
70 West Hubbard #205
Chicago, IL 60610

JoyCe Stolberg Interiors Inc.
2205 NE 207 Street
N. Miami Beach, FL 33150
305/931.6010
Fax: 305/931.6040

J. Powell and Associates, Inc.
100 W. Beaver Creek Blvd.
PO Box 1641
Avon, CO 81620
970/845.7731
Fax: 970/845.8903
e-mail: jpowell@vail.net

Julie Lanterman Interior Designs
5 St. Francis Road
Hillsborough, CA
650/348.3823
Fax: 650/348.3823

J. Westerfield Antiques
& Interiors, Inc.
4429 Old Canton Road
Jackson, MS 39211
601/362.7508
Fax: 601/366.4718

Kathleen Buoymaster, Inc.
6933 La Jolla Blvd.
La Jolla, CA 92037
619/456.2850
Fax: 619/456.0672

Klingmans of Grand Rapids
3525 28th Street, SE
Grand Rapids, MI 49512
616/942.7300
Fax: 616/942.1957

Kuckly Associates
506 E. 74th Street
New York, NY 10021
212/772.2228
Fax: 212/772.2130

Kuhl Design Associates
5100 Westheimer, Suite 200
Houston, TX 77056
713/840.1500
Fax: 713/840.1318
e-mail: pekuhl@aol.com

Laura Bohn Design Associates, Inc.
30 W 26 Street
New York, NY 10010
212/645.3636
Fax: 212/645.3639

Lovick Design
11339 Bumham Street
Los Angeles, CA 90049

Lynn Robinson Interiors
Powers Building
34 Audrey Avenue
Oyster Bay, NY 11771
615/921.4455
Fax: 615/921.8163

Margot S. Wilson
4305 Westover Place N.W.
Washington, D.C. 20016
202/244.2171
Fax: 202/363.6647

Michael deSantis, Inc.
1110 Second Avenue
New York, NY 10022

Meadowbank Designs Inc.
Box 165
Bryn Mawr, PA 19010
610/525.4909
Fax: 610/525.3909

M. L. Slovack Design, Inc.
7610 Bryonwood
Houston, TX 77055
713/956.7240
Fax: 713/682.7184

Myrl Talkington Designs
6915 Tokolm
Dallas, TX 75214
214/328.9942
Fax: 214/321.4067

Nicholson Interiors
1810 West 35th Street
Austin, TX 78703
512/458.6395
Fax: 512/467.2050

Pedlar's Village Interior Design
3562 S. Osprey Avenue
Sarasota, FL 34239
941/955.5726
Fax: 941/366.9563

Ron Hefler
465 South Sweetzer Avenue
Los Angeles, CA 90048
213/651.1231
Fax: 213/735.2502

Rodgers Menzies Interior Design
766 South White Station Road
Memphis, TN 38117
901/761.3161
Fax: 901/763.3993

Samantha Cole & Company
550 15th Street
San Francisco, CA 94103
415/864.0100
Fax: 415/864.5333

S & B Interiors Inc.
11270 SW 59th Avenue
Miami, FL 33156
305/661.1572
Fax: 305/661.2722
e-mail: sandb@herald.infi.net

Samuel Botero Associates
420 East 54th Street
Suite 346
New York, NY 10022

Sandra Nunnerley Inc.
112 East 71st Street
New York, NY 10021
212/472.9341
Fax: 212/472.9346

Scott Salvator Inc.
308 East 79th Street
New York, NY 10021
212/861.5355
Fax: 212/861.9557

Stedila Design
135 East 55th Street
New York, NY 10022
212/751.4281
Fax: 212/751.6698

Stingray Hornsby Interior Design
5 The Green
Watertown, CT 06795
860/274.2293
Fax: 860/945.3369
e-mail: stingray@snet.net

Sue Wenk Interior Design
300 East 71st Street
New York, NY 10021
212/879.5149

Susan Kroeger, Ltd.
890 Green Bay Road
Winnetka, IL 60093
847/441.0346
Fax: 847/441.0356

Tonin MacCallum ASID Inc.
21 E 90
New York City, NY 10128
212/831.8909
Fax: 212/427.2069

Trilogy
Village Green
Bedford, NY 10506
914/234.3071
Fax: 914/234.0540

Thurston Kitchen and Bath
2920 E 6th Avenue
Denver, CO 80206
303/399.4564
Fax: 303/399.3179

V-3 Design
1212 Avenue of Americas, #802
New York, NY 10036
212/222.2551
Fax: 212/222.2201

～ Index ～

"In *Don't Pick On Me*, Susan Eikov Green makes it easy for kids to understand, and act on feelings associated with bullying. Through clear language and straightforward explanations, Don't Pick on Me also arms kids with concrete techniques for dealing with bullying and building confidence."

—Aimee Lichtenfeld, LCSW, clinical school social worker in New York City

"Susan Eikov Green has written a practical and compassionate book on a difficult subject. Parents, teachers, and clinicians will find it a valuable resource for helping children acquire security and success from the inside out."

—Christopher McCurry, Ph.D., author of *Parenting Your Anxious Child with Mindfulness and Acceptance*

Don't Pick On Me

Help for Kids to Stand Up to
& Deal with Bullies

SUSAN EIKOV GREEN

Instant Help Books
A Division of New Harbinger Publications, Inc.

Distributed in Canada by Raincoast Books

Copyright © 2010 by Susan Eikov Green
        Instant Help Books
        A Division of New Harbinger Publications, Inc.
        5674 Shattuck Avenue
        Oakland, CA 94609
        www.newharbinger.com

Cover design by Amy Shoup
Interior illustrations by Julie Olsen
Cover photograph is a model used for illustrative purposes only.

FSC
Mixed Sources
Product group from well-managed
forests and other controlled sources
Cert no. SW-COC-002283
www.fsc.org
© 1996 Forest Stewardship Council

Library of Congress Cataloging-in-Publication Data

Green, Susan.
  Don't pick on me : help for kids to stand up to and deal with bullies / by Susan Eikov Green.
    p. cm.
  ISBN 978-1-57224-713-0
  1. Bullying--Juvenile literature. 2. Bullying--Prevention--Juvenile literature. 3. Cyberbullying--Juvenile literature. I. Title.
  BF637.B85G74 2010
  303.6'9--dc22

                          2009051825

12   11   10

10   9   8   7   6   5   4   3   2   1

First Printing

TABLE OF CONTENTS

Introduction

Is bullying being hit or punched? Is it being teased and made fun of? Is it being picked on by kids who are bigger than you? Is it being talked about behind your back? Is it being called a name that really bothers you? Is it being embarrassed or made to feel foolish or just plain scared? Actually, bullying is all of those things and more.

Everyone comes up against a bully at one time or another. It's almost impossible not to, because there are lots of kids who act like bullies. Most kids who bully want to feel like they are in control. Bullying makes them feel powerful and important. Some kids bully because they've been bullied themselves, maybe by a brother, sister, or parent. They think that's the way to act. Some kids bully because they think it will help them be popular by making them the center of attention.

How can you recognize a bully? Well, not all bullies look the same, so you can't tell who is a bully just by looking, but you can tell by how they act.

If you think bullying is something you just have to take and not do anything about, then think again. Because you don't have to put up with bullying. No one does. And that's what this book is all about. The activities it contains will show you different strategies for dealing with bullies and help you learn how to put those strategies to work for you.

Now, let's get going. And when you're finished with the activities in this book, you'll be able to say:

Don't pick on me! I know how to handle bullying!

For You to Know

A bully is someone who picks on, teases, or physically hurts another person. Most people—kids and adults alike—have come up against bullies. It's almost impossible not to.

There are all kinds of bullies, and not all bullying is the same. Some bullies use words to hurt kids. They tease or name-call or threaten.

Like Danielle: *She calls Olivia "Porky Pig" because Olivia is a little overweight.*

Some bullies spread rumors or leave kids out and get others to ignore them too.

Like Nicole: *She doesn't like Robert because he is good at math and she isn't. So she spread the rumor that Robert cheated on the math test.*

Some bullies punch or hit or shove. Or they take and destroy things that don't belong to them.

Like Eddie: *He goes out his way to push Willy when they're walking down the stairs.*

Not all bullies pick on kids they don't like. There are some who like to bully their friends.

Like Wanda: *She wants her friends to do things her way. She thought Lutecia wasn't following her "rules," so she stopped talking to her and got their other friends to stop talking to her too.*

Let's see if you have a bully in your life who causes problems for you or someone else.

For You to Do

How often do you come into contact with a bully? The bully may be someone who picks on you or someone who picks on other kids. Check the column to say if the answer is "Often," "Sometimes," or "Never."

Did you ever see anyone:	Often	Sometimes	Never
give a kid a mean nickname?	_____	_____	_____
take someone's lunch?	_____	_____	_____
leave someone out on purpose?	_____	_____	_____
spread a rumor?	_____	_____	_____
tease someone about the way he or she looks?	_____	_____	_____
embarrass someone just to make other kids laugh?	_____	_____	_____
call a kid a "funny" name after being asked not to?	_____	_____	_____
play a mean trick on another kid?	_____	_____	_____
pick on a kid he knew wouldn't fight back?	_____	_____	_____
hit someone out of anger?	_____	_____	_____
take another kid's property and destroy it on purpose?	_____	_____	_____
get other kids to gang up on a smaller or weaker kid?	_____	_____	_____
get other kids to stop talking to someone else?	_____	_____	_____
tell another kid, "You better watch out!"	_____	_____	_____

Tell whether bullying is a big problem for you, and why.

_____

_____

_____

... And More to Do

It's good to know where you might see a bully so you won't be taken by surprise. How often have you seen bullying happen in these places?

1 = hardly ever; 2 = sometimes; 3 = often

At the bus stop	1	2	3
On the school bus	1	2	3
In the classroom	1	2	3
In the lunchroom	1	2	3
In the school bathroom	1	2	3
In the park	1	2	3
On the playground	1	2	3
At home	1	2	3

Can you think of other places where you might see a bully? If you can, write them down here and rate them.

_____	1	2	3
_____	1	2	3
_____	1	2	3

For You to Know

Being bullied can bring on many different feelings. Giving your feelings a name is the first step in being able to deal with them.

When someone picks on you, you might think, "I feel bad." But "bad" doesn't really say very much. "Bad" can be the way you describe everything from having a stomachache to flunking a test to breaking your mother's favorite picture frame.

Being picked on can certainly bring on lots of different feelings, and there are many, many words you can use to describe these feelings.

Isabella felt nervous when she went to the girls' room. She was afraid that Kaitlyn would be there and try to pull her hair.

Adam felt embarrassed when Dylan made fun of the way he ran.

Jasmine felt lonely and hurt when Ava and her friends wouldn't let her sit with them at lunch.

Giving your feelings a name will help you deal with what's bothering you. It's important to learn how to recognize and deal with your feelings so that they don't get bottled up inside.

For You to Do

Column A shows a list of feelings you may have had if you've been bullied. Column B shows definitions for each feeling. Draw a line from the word in Column A to the correct definition in Column B. If you don't know the answer, look it up in a dictionary.

Column A	Column B
lonely	ill; achy
confused	jittery
embarrassed	fearful
sad	silly
angry	guilty
hurt	frightened; afraid
worried	unhappy
scared	ill at ease; flustered
foolish	mad; not pleased; enraged
ashamed	upset; offended
nervous	mixed-up; bewildered
sick	without a friend

How a Bully Makes You Feel: Sad, Scared, and More

Can you think of any other feelings bullying can cause? If you can, write them down here.

_____   _____   _____

_____   _____   _____

_____   _____   _____

_____   _____   _____

... And More to Do

Read these situations that involve kids who are being picked on. Then write down the name of the feeling you would have if you were the one being bullied. You can use one of the feelings listed on the previous page, or any others you can think of.

Luis walks into his classroom and sits down at his desk. He quickly jumps up because someone has left a puddle of water on his seat! The other kids see this and laugh.

How would you feel if you were Luis?

_____

Mindy got a new bike for her birthday and she's very proud of it. When some older kids see her riding it, they make fun of the bike and start calling her "Baby Wheels."

How would you feel if you were Mindy?

_____

Jesse is shooting hoops in his driveway when his older brother Will gets home. Will tells Jesse to go inside because he and his friends are going to play basketball. Jesse says, "It's not fair. I was here first." Will answers, "Tough. Leave now or you'll be sorry."

How would you feel if you were Jesse?

_____

Shelby and Christy are good friends. They usually sit together on the bus, but for the past few days, Christy has been sitting with another girl. When Shelby asks why, Christy doesn't answer. She pretends that Shelby isn't even there.

How would you feel if you were Shelby?

_____

The students in Ms. Barker's class have been divided into groups to organize a party. Jan is in the group deciding how to decorate the classroom, but the other kids in the group won't include her or ask what she wants to do. They even plan meetings without telling her.

How would you feel if you were Jan?

_____

For You to Know

Bullying can also affect your body. When someone picks on you, it can bring on many different physical feelings.

Bullying can bring a lot of feelings, like anger or sadness or fear. It can also bring on physical feelings, like a headache or a stomachache. Has that ever happened to you?

What you are feeling is stress. When you are worried or frightened or uncomfortable, you feel stress. And stress can cause more than just headaches or stomachaches. Some kids get rashes when they are stressed. Some kids have trouble catching their breath, and some kids find it hard to sleep.

When you are stressed, there are ways you can help yourself feel better.

For You to Do

Here are some of the physical reactions some kids have to being picked on. Put a check in the column that shows how often each one happens to you. If there any other physical feelings that you have, add them to the list.

When I get picked on, I get:

	Often	Sometimes	Never
a stomachache	＿＿	＿＿	＿＿
a headache	＿＿	＿＿	＿＿
hot and start to sweat	＿＿	＿＿	＿＿
cold and start to shiver	＿＿	＿＿	＿＿
nauseated and feel like I'm going to vomit	＿＿	＿＿	＿＿
very tense	＿＿	＿＿	＿＿
dizzy	＿＿	＿＿	＿＿
short of breath	＿＿	＿＿	＿＿
achy all over	＿＿	＿＿	＿＿
＿＿＿＿＿＿＿＿＿＿	＿＿	＿＿	＿＿
＿＿＿＿＿＿＿＿＿＿	＿＿	＿＿	＿＿
＿＿＿＿＿＿＿＿＿＿	＿＿	＿＿	＿＿

... *And More to Do*

Taking your mind off what is bothering you is a great way to deal with stress. Here are some things you can do if stress makes you feel sick. Put a check to show whether you think any of these strategies would help you.

	A Lot	A Little	Not My Thing
Take a few deep breaths.	____	____	____
Count to ten until you are calm.	____	____	____
Close your eyes and think of something calm and relaxing.	____	____	____
Go for a run.	____	____	____
Shoot some hoops.	____	____	____
Ride a bike.	____	____	____
Go skating.	____	____	____
Play an instrument.	____	____	____
Talk to a friend.	____	____	____
Read a book.	____	____	____
Listen to music.	____	____	____

Can you think of any other things you could try? Write them here.

_____

_____

_____

Activity 4   Look Brave, Act Brave

For You to Know

Bullies like to pick on kids who look and act afraid. If you can put on a brave face and act confident, a bully might just pass you by.

The way you look and act sends out a message to kids who might be thinking about bullying you.

> *Every day when Brandon gets to school, one of the first kids he sees is Mickey. Mickey is big and loud and scary, and Brandon is afraid of him. So whenever Brandon sees Mickey, he walks with his head down or turned away, and he hopes that Mickey won't notice him. But Mickey does see Brandon, and what he sees is someone he thinks would be easy to pick on.*

Brandon doesn't realize that he is sending out a message to Mickey. The message he's sending is: "I'm afraid of you." And for some bullies, that's a signal that says, "I bet this kid is somebody I can pick on."

So what can Brandon do? He can change the way he looks and acts. That doesn't mean that he won't still *be* frightened. It means that he won't *act* frightened. He won't send out the message that says: "I'm someone who would be easy for you to pick on." Instead, he'll send out the message that says, " Don't pick on me."

And that might just stop the bullying before it can start!

For You to Do

Did you know that your body has a way of "talking"? It's called body language. Even though it doesn't use any words, your body language says a lot about you.

What do you think the body language of these two kids is saying? Put an X through the one whose body is saying: "I'm afraid." Circle the one whose body is saying: "Don't pick on me."

When you look down, frown, slouch, and fidget, your body is saying: "I'm afraid of you."

When you make eye contact, smile, and stand tall and still, your body is saying: "I'm brave, not afraid."

Remember, that doesn't mean you don't feel afraid. It means that you don't look afraid. And that can do a lot to keep a bully away from you.

So try it out. Stand in front of a mirror or practice with someone else. Stand straight. Don't fidget. Put on a smile. And look the person you're facing right in the eye.

... *And More to Do*

One thing that can help you look brave and act brave is self-talk. Self-talk is just what it sounds like. It is a way of talking to yourself, but in your head, like a quiet conversation between you and your inner voice. You can use self-talk to remind yourself to look and act brave.

When you get on the bus or walk down the hall or go into your classroom, you can use self-talk. You can do it when you sit in the lunchroom, play in the park, or go into gym class, as well. Wherever you are, you can help yourself with messages like these.

"She's scary, but I'm not going to let her see how I feel."

"Don't mess with me."

"Stand up tall."

"Smile."

"I'm okay—I can do this."

"Put on a brave face."

"It's okay to be nervous, but I'm not going to show him."

Put a check next to the self-talk statements you think might work for you. Write down some other things that you could say to yourself to help you look and act brave. Then practice saying them.

Activity 5   Look Good, Feel Good

> ## *For You to Know*
>
> The way you look—your appearance—says a lot about you.
> Having a clean, healthy appearance not only makes you look
> good, it also helps you feel more confident.

In Activity 4, you found out that your body language says a lot about you. Well, so does your appearance. Your appearance is the way you look. It's the *you* that other people see. Looking good not only tells other people that you are confident, it makes you feel more confident about yourself. Because looking good makes you feel good!

> Like Haley: *Her hair is always combed, her hands and nails are clean, and her clothing is neat. And then there's Laura. She usually forgets to tie her shoelaces. Her hair always looks messy, and she often has dirty hands.*

Which girl do you think is more likely to be picked on? Remember, bullies usually pick on kids who don't look confident. And looking good and feeling good can give you a lot of confidence in yourself.

For You to Do

Practicing good personal hygiene is the best way to look good. Good hygiene means taking care of your body and developing healthy habits so you look clean and smell clean too. How do you rate?

Do you:	Always	Sometimes	Not So Often
brush your teeth at least twice a day?	_____	_____	_____
take a shower or a bath daily?	_____	_____	_____
wash your hair regularly?	_____	_____	_____
wear clean clothes?	_____	_____	_____
change your underwear every day?	_____	_____	_____
comb your hair?	_____	_____	_____
keep your hands and fingernails clean?	_____	_____	_____

As you get older, there's more to personal hygiene.

If you have started puberty, do you also:

	Always	Sometimes	Not So Often
use deodorant?	_____	_____	_____
wash your face with soap to prevent zits?	_____	_____	_____
wash your feet before you go to bed?	_____	_____	_____

How do you rate? Do you need to improve in any of these areas? If you do, set a goal to do it. Write your goal here:

_____

_____

... And More to Do

By keeping track of your personal hygiene to be sure your appearance is clean and neat, you can help yourself feel good and be confident. Use this chart for one week of school. You can also make copies of the chart and keep track of your appearance for as many weeks as you like.

Monday	*Tuesday*	*Wednesday*	*Thursday*	*Friday*
☐ I brushed my teeth.	☐ I brushed my teeth.	☐ I brushed my teeth.	☐ I brushed my teeth.	☐ I brushed my teeth.
☐ I took a bath or shower.	☐ I took a bath or shower.	☐ I took a bath or shower.	☐ I took a bath or shower.	☐ I took a bath or shower.
☐ My hair is clean and combed.	☐ My hair is clean and combed.	☐ My hair is clean and combed.	☐ My hair is clean and combed.	☐ My hair is clean and combed.
☐ I'm wearing clean underwear.	☐ I'm wearing clean underwear.	☐ I'm wearing clean underwear.	☐ I'm wearing clean underwear.	☐ I'm wearing clean underwear.
☐ My clothes are clean and neat.	☐ My clothes are clean and neat.	☐ My clothes are clean and neat.	☐ My clothes are clean and neat.	☐ My clothes are clean and neat.
☐ My shoelaces are tied.	☐ My shoelaces are tied.	☐ My shoelaces are tied.	☐ My shoelaces are tied.	☐ My shoelaces are tied.
☐ I look good.	☐ I look good.	☐ I look good.	☐ I look good.	☐ I look good.
☐ I feel good.	☐ I feel good.	☐ I feel good.	☐ I feel good.	☐ I feel good.
☐ I am confident!	☐ I am confident!	☐ I am confident!	☐ I am confident!	☐ I am confident!

For You to Know

Bullies who pick on you like it when you get angry or upset. It gives them the satisfaction of knowing that whatever they did got to you. So if someone picks on you, it's important to try not to let your feelings show.

Matt was riding his bike in the park. He had left his jacket and water bottle near a tree. After a while, he stopped to take a drink from the bottle. He took a big gulp and then spit the water out. Someone had dumped salt into it! He looked over and saw Judd laughing at him. Then other kids started to laugh, especially when they saw that Matt had water all over his shirt and pants. Matt was so embarrassed that he started to cry. That made everyone laugh even harder.

Tara was in the library reading a book when Becky sat down and started to annoy her. First Becky tapped her fingers on the table. Then she moved her chair so close that Tara had no room to move. She began to swing her feet and kick Tara under the table. Finally Tara couldn't take any more. "Stop doing that," she yelled. But Becky didn't stop. "I hate you!" Tara shouted. Becky still didn't say anything. She just looked at Tara with a big grin on her face.

Matt and Tara let their feelings show. By crying, Matt let Judd know that his bullying had upset him. By yelling and shouting, Tara gave Becky the satisfaction of knowing that what she did really bothered her. It isn't that Matt and Tara shouldn't feel the way they do, but by letting the bullies see those feelings, they made it more likely that they would be picked on again.

For You to Do

If someone is bullying you, before you yell, cry, explode, or react in any other way, take some time to cool down. Get control of yourself and try not to let the bully see how you feel.

Here are a few things you can do to help you cool down:

- Take a few deep, long, sl-o-o-o-w breaths.

- Count to ten. 12345678910

- Say the alphabet to yourself. You can say it forward from A to Z or backward from Z to A.

- Think of something calm and peaceful.

- Think of the people who love you.

- Think of things you like to do.

What else could you do that would help you to relax and cool down?

I could: _____.

I could: _____.

I could: _____.

I could: _____.

Now practice. Close your eyes. Imagine that you are Matt or Tara, or think of a time when you felt like they did. Pick one of the ideas from the list. Keep at it until you are calm and cool.

Practicing will make it a lot easier to not react when the time comes. When you are cool and calm, you'll be in control of yourself. And then you'll be better able to deal with any situation and figure out what to do.

... *And More to Do*

Not showing your feelings to a bully doesn't mean that you have to hide them forever. It's important to let your feelings out. Keeping them bottled up inside could give you the aches and pains you read about in Activity 3. So once you're away from the bully and in a safe place, you can try some of these ways to let your feelings out. Put a circle around the ideas you think would help you.

Talk to someone.	Ask for help.	Take a walk.
Ride a bike.	Shoot hoops.	Bang a drum.
Write in a journal.	Draw a picture.	Play with a friend.
Go for a run.	Hit a pillow.	Throw a ball against a wall.
Dance.	Play a game.	Bounce a ball.

Can you think of any others? Write them here.

_____   _____   _____

_____   _____   _____

Once you let your feelings out, you'll be able to manage them in healthy ways, and you won't give the bully the satisfaction of knowing that the bullying worked.

For You to Know

When someone picks on you, your first reaction might be to do to the bully whatever the bully did to you. But that will only make things worse.

For some kids, fighting back can be almost automatic.

Britney purposely ran into Lara on the playground and knocked her down. Lara was mad. She got up and ran after Britney, then pushed her down. Britney came right back at Lara, and soon the girls were in a big fight.

Anthony called Austin "Fatso," so Austin called Anthony "Stupid." Then Anthony called Austin "Fat pig," and Austin called Anthony "Super stupid." Next Anthony pushed Austin, and Austin pushed Anthony back.

Doing what a bully does to you won't make that bully go away. In fact, it usually makes the bullying worse. And it makes the bully feel good too. Because when you react that way, you're letting the bully know that what he or she has done has gotten to you. That's what the bully is looking for. And when you fight back, you're just prolonging the bullying. That's not what you want. You want the bullying to stop.

Another good reason for not bullying back is that you could get hurt. Most bullies are bigger and stronger than the kids they pick on—and they know it.

Need one more reason? There's a good chance you'll get in trouble.

Not bullying back doesn't mean you have to put up with a bully. It just means that you shouldn't do to the bully whatever the bully has done to you. Instead, when someone starts picking on you, find a healthy way to cool down.

For You to Do

What do you think might happen to Lara if she keeps fighting with Britney?

_____

_____

What do you think Lara could do to cool down?

_____

_____

How do you think that would help?

_____

_____

What do you think might happen to Austin if he keeps fighting with Anthony?

_____

_____

What do you think Austin could do to cool down?

_____

_____

How do you think that would help?

_____

_____

... And More to Do

Think of a time you fought back when a bully picked on you. If that has never happened, think of a time when you saw another kid fight back, and answer these questions as if you were that kid.

What happened?

_____

_____

_____

Did fighting back make the situation better or worse?

_____

Did you get hurt?

_____

Did you get in trouble?

_____

What could you have done to cool down?

_____

_____

> ## For You to Know
>
> The best way to deal with bullies is not to come into contact with them in the first place. Whenever possible, stay as far away from a bully as you can.

Where do you see bullies? On the bus? On the way to school? On the playground? In the lunchroom? Those are some of the places where bullying is most likely to happen. Here are some ideas to help you avoid bullies in those places:

On the bus

If a certain kid on the bus always picks on you, try to get a seat as far away as you can. Sitting close to the driver can be a big help.

On the way to school

If you pass a bully on the way to school, see if you can find another way to go. If you can't find another route, then walk on the other side of the street. Try to put as much space as you can between you and the bully. And walk with a friend, if you can. Bullies tend to pick on kids who are alone.

On the playground

Look for a place to play where the bully doesn't hang out. Don't pick a place where you'll be by yourself. Be sure there are other people around.

In the lunchroom

Bullies often hang out together at lunch time. Sit at a table that is as far away from that bunch as possible. Pick a spot that's close to the teacher or the aide in charge, and sit with a friend.

It isn't always possible to avoid a bully, but try to do that whenever you can.

For You to Do

To get to the library, these kids have to go through the park, where a mean bully hangs out. Can you help them find a way to the library without passing the bully?

... *And More to Do*

Fill in the blanks to help these kids steer clear of the bullies they see.

Antonio took his markers and a drawing pad to the playground so he could sit at the table and draw. That's what he liked to do at recess. But today he noticed that Andy and Rodrigo were playing a game at the table. Andy and Rodrigo always teased Antonio because he liked to draw. So Antonio ...

_____

Sela usually ate lunch with her friends Marlee and Taylor. But today Marlee was absent and Taylor was sitting with a girl who liked to tease Sela and call her funny names. Then Sela noticed Becca sitting at a table by herself. Becca and Sela weren't friends, but Sela knew that Becca was very nice. As Sela was trying to decide where to sit, Taylor waved to her. Sela thought for a minute about where she should sit, and then she ...

_____

As Pete was walking down the hall on his way to the boys' bathroom on the first floor, he saw two boys who he knew were bullies go in. There were bathrooms on every floor, so Pete ...

_____

When Julia came into the auditorium for a special show, she saw that there were only two empty seats. One seat was right next to a teacher. The other seat was between Jordan, a boy who liked to pick on Julia, and a girl from another class she didn't know. Julia decided to ...

_____

Activity 9

Assertive, Aggressive, or Passive

For You to Know

Being assertive is a way of standing up for yourself. When you are assertive, your tone of voice is firm but friendly. Your body language shows you are confident. And your words let a bully know that you aren't someone who will be easy to pick on.

There are three ways that people talk, look, and act. One way is being assertive. Being assertive means that you stand up tall, you look the person you are talking to right in the eye, and you use words that match the message you are trying to send. You show the bully that you are confident. You stand up for your rights without stepping on the rights of others.

Another way is being aggressive. When you're aggressive, you go on the attack, which might make the bully angry. You may end up in a fight.

Sometimes kids who are bullied behave in a third way—they are passive. If you are passive, your body language says you're afraid. You don't speak in a firm, respectful voice; instead, your tone is wishy-washy, and you hint at what you mean but don't come out and say it directly You don't act and sound like you mean what you're saying, so the bully probably won't take you seriously.

Acting aggressively or passively may just make the bullying worse. Acting assertively lets a bully know that you mean what you say: you want the bullying to stop!

For You to Do

Read the story below and decide whether the behavior is aggressive, assertive, or passive. Then tell what you think happened next.

Manny, Timmy, and Gretchen had come to the basketball game early so they could get the best seats. When Reggie came in, he decided that none of the open seats were good enough. He was going to get a better one—whether the kid already sitting there liked it or not!

When Reggie tried to push Manny off of the bench, Manny looked him right in the eye and said, "Please don't push me. I'm sitting here." Manny is being:

aggressive   assertive   passive

What do you think happened next?

_____

_____

When Reggie tried to push Timmy off the bench, Timmy looked down at his feet and said "Oh … um … I … um … really wanted to sit here." Timmy is being:

aggressive   assertive   passive

What do you think happened next?

_____

_____

When Reggie tried to push Gretchen off the bench, Gretchen pushed him back and said, "Hey, who do you think you're pushing!" Gretchen is being:

aggressive   assertive   passive

What do you think happened next?

_____

_____

... *And More to Do*

Read these things that you can say to a bully who is calling you names. Circle the ones that are assertive. Put a line through the ones that are aggressive and an X over the ones that are passive.

Please stop. I don't like when you say that to me.

You're such a jerk to say that.

It bothers me when people act the way you do.

If you say that again, you're going to be sorry!

I don't think that's funny, so please stop.

Get out of my face, big mouth!

Um ... I don't think that's so nice.

Why do people have to call each other names?

Please stop calling me that name.

Cut it out, stupid!

For You to Know

When a bully does mean things to you—calls you names or teases you or puts you down or plays a nasty prank on you—you can stand up for yourself by speaking confidently. Let the bully know that you want the bullying to stop.

In earlier activities, you learned that looking and acting brave and using self-talk can help you when you are being bullied. You can also help yourself by learning how to speak confidently. Here are some tips that will make it easier for you to stand up for yourself and be assertive when you talk to a bully:

- Look the bully right in the eye.

- Use a firm but friendly tone of voice. Don't sound wishy-washy or angry.

- Speak in a voice that can be heard. Don't shout but don't whisper.

- Let the bully know that you are serious about what you say.

- Don't get into an argument or a fight. Be respectful.

- Keep it short. Don't get into a discussion.

- When you have said what you want to say, walk away.

Remember, don't push, shove, or hit, and try not to let your feelings show. Act confident. Bullies tend to pick on kids who don't stand up for themselves.

For You to Do

When it comes to standing up for yourself and being assertive, it's important to be aware of your tone of voice. That means the way you say something. You can say the same words, and how they sound to others will change depending on your tone of voice. Try this:

Say, "I don't want to"

- being firm but polite;

- being annoyed;

- being angry.

Now say, "Stop it"

- being firm but polite;

- being annoyed;

- being angry.

Next try, "Stay away from me"

- being firm but polite;

- being annoyed;

- being angry.

Notice how different it sounds each time. You can make a listener know how you feel and what you mean just by your tone of voice. So when you stand up to a bully, make your tone of voice firm, but not angry. Make sure you sound like you mean what you're saying.

... And More to Do

Practicing helps too. It will make you feel more confident. So practice saying:

- "Stop it."

- "I want you to stop saying that to me."

- "Don't do that again."

- "Please stay away from me."

- "Leave me alone."

- "Don't pick on me."

It also helps if you practice with someone else—maybe a parent or an older brother or sister. Pretend that you're rehearsing your lines for a play. That will make it more fun. Here's your script:

Bully: Hey, twinkletoes, I hear you're taking dancing lessons.

You: Please don't call me that.

Bully: You eat the most disgusting things for lunch.

You: That's not very nice. Please don't say it again.

Bully: You are such a dummy. You can't do anything right.

You: I don't like it when you talk to me that way.

Bully: You mind if I just take a peek at your homework and maybe copy one or two things?

You: Yes, I mind. Please leave me alone.

Activity 11

There's Safety in Numbers

> ### *For You to Know*
>
> Bullies usually like to pick on kids who are alone. Being with other kids will make it less likely that a bully will come after you.

The saying "There's safety in numbers" is certainly true when it comes to bullying. For the most part, bullies find it easier to pick on kids who are by themselves.

That's what Rosa found out. When Rosa walked home from school, Jason would walk behind her. He'd step up close to Rosa and pull her hair and whisper in her ear. It was annoying, and even worse, it made Rosa feel nervous. Then she started walking home with her friends Abby and Casey. From that day on, Jason stopped picking on Rosa.

Find a friend or friends who will give you support. But make sure you and your friends don't act like a gang. Never use violence. It's not about taking anyone on or evening up the sides—you're just finding a way to get support and protection so you can feel safe.

For You to Do

Devon is alone on the playground when Steven, a bully in his class, comes along. Complete this picture to show how Devon could be safer.

... And More to Do

Do you have friends that you can count on? Do you feel more secure when you are with your friends? Write about a time when being with a friend or friends made you feel safer.

_____

_____

_____

_____

_____

_____

_____

_____

_____

_____

_____

For You to Know

Bullies like to be the boss and get attention. But if you don't react, a bully might just give up and leave you alone.

When Cori waited for the bus in the morning, Arianna always had something nasty to say: "I bet you couldn't do the math homework." "Where did you get that coat!" "Are you going to sit with that jerky kid?"

What Arianna said really bothered Cori. She didn't like it, and it made her feel uncomfortable and nervous. Cori told her sister Stephanie about Arianna, and Stephanie told her that she should try to ignore Arianna. "Just act like you didn't hear a thing," Stephanie said.

And that's what Cori did. She pretended that she didn't hear Arianna at all. No matter what Arianna said, Cori acted like she didn't even notice. And pretty soon Arianna gave up. Picking on Cori wasn't fun anymore.

Activity 12

For You to Do

When you try to ignore a bully, self-talk can really help. It can get you on the right path.
So if someone is picking on you, your inner voice can say:

"I'm not going to listen to that!"   "I'm pretending I don't hear you."

"Who's he talking to? Not me."   "Keep walking."

"Act like she isn't here."   "It's okay to be nervous, but I can handle this."

Write in what the boy in this picture could say to himself to help him ignore the bully.

Don't Pick on Me

... And More to Do

Think of a time when you tried to ignore a bully. If that hasn't happened to you, think of a time when you saw another kid do it, and answer these questions as if you were that kid.

What did you do?

_____

_____

What happened as a result?

_____

_____

If you tried self-talk, what did your inner voice say?

_____

_____

If you didn't use self-talk, what could your inner voice have said?

_____

_____

Do you think that would have helped you?

_____

_____

Will you try self-talk next time?

_____

_____

> ### *For You to Know*
>
> An I-message is an assertive way to talk about your feelings. If the bully is someone you think you can talk to, using an I-message to explain how you feel can be a good strategy to try.

An I-message lets you say how you feel, what makes you feel that way, and what you would like the other person to do. It is a good way to communicate without putting down the other person or starting a fight.

The message always begins with the words "I feel ..." For example, if your brother put you down in front of your friends, you could say:

"I feel embarrassed when you make me look silly in front of my friends. I want you to promise not to do that again."

Or if someone is making fun of your shoes, you could say:

"I feel silly when you make fun of my shoes. I want you to stop saying things like that to me."

In addition to using I-messages, remember these other tips from earlier activities:

- Find a place to talk that is out in the open, where other people can see you.

- Look the bully right in the eye. Look brave and act brave.

- Be assertive. Make sure your body language, tone of voice, and the words you use send the message that you want the bully to hear: "Don't pick on me."

- Don't yell or shout or lose your temper—no put-downs, no insults. And don't get into a fight.

- Practice ahead of time. Practice over and over until you feel confident.

For You to Do

Read these situations, and then write an I-message for each kid who is being bullied.

Just before gym class, Peter has to go to the nurse's office to take his asthma medicine so that he won't get out of breath when he runs around. Once he takes the medicine he's fine, but Ned likes to cough and pretend that he can't catch his breath just to make fun of Peter.

Peter could say: I feel _____ when you _____.

I want you to _____.

Mia and her older sister Lauren share a computer. Whenever Mia is using the computer and Lauren wants it, she tells Mia that she has to stop whatever she's doing right away. She says that because she's older than Mia, her work is more important.

Mia could say: I feel _____ when you _____.

I want you to _____.

Kyle tried out for a part in the school play. He wanted the lead but he got only a small role. Emily made fun of him for being disappointed. She said that Kyle wasn't as good as the kid who got the lead and that he should be happy he got any part at all.

Kyle could say: I feel _____ when you _____.

I want you to _____.

... And More to Do

Think of a time when using an I-message could have helped you with a bully. Write the message you might have used here:

_____

_____

_____

Then stand in front of a mirror and practice saying your message. Be sure your body language and tone of voice match your words.

How did you feel using an I-message?

_____

_____

For You to Know

Having something funny to say to a bully, like a joke or a good comeback, may help to calm down a hot situation.

Turning the tables on a bully by making a joke or having a good comeback can sometimes stop the bullying. It's a really good thing to try, because it's better to have someone laugh *with* you than laugh *at* you.

Here are some examples:

Kelly: *Where did you get that ridiculous shirt?*

Max: *You think this is ridiculous? You should see my other shirt.*

Rachel: *That haircut is so ugly.*

Libby: *Thanks for noticing.*

Bobby: *I can't believe you dropped the ball.*

Gary: *I can't believe it either!*

You will probably have to think of some things to say ahead of time. Just be sure that whatever you say to the bully isn't an insult or a put-down. For example, it would have been insulting if Libby had said to Rachel, "You think my haircut is ugly? I guess you didn't look in the mirror this morning" or if Gary had told Bobby, "I was trying to imitate you. That's why I dropped the ball!" And don't say anything that will embarrass the bully in front of others. You want to stop the bullying, not make things worse.

For You to Do

What could you say in each of these situations? Try to think of a joke or a good comeback that will stop the bullying before it gets going. If you need some help, ask a friend or family member to give you a hand.

Bully: You are such a dummy. I can't wait to tell everyone you got a C– on that test.

You: _____.

Bully: You like that kid? That must be because you have no other friends.

You: _____.

Bully: You are the worst soccer player. I only hope we're not on the same team.

You: _____.

Bully: You call that singing? It sounds like a fire alarm.

You: _____.

Bully: That new band you like—they are the worst! There has to be something wrong with you.

You: _____.

Bully: You're such a klutz! Who else would fall getting off the bus?

You: _____.

... And More to Do

It can be just as hard to "deliver" a joke or a good comeback as it is to think of one. That's why comedians and actors spend so much time rehearsing. So take the lines you came up with, and rehearse them. Do it in front of a mirror or get someone to play the other part. And get an audience together if you can. Make sure your body language and tone of voice match what you're saying.

Practicing your lines will make you feel more confident when the time comes to use one of them.

Activity 15   "I'm Out of Here!"

For You to Know

One thing is for sure—no one can pick on you if you aren't there. So when a bully comes for you, walk away if you can. That's especially true if the situation is dangerous.

Sometimes your body tells you when you are in danger. Your heart might start to beat very fast and you might get very jittery. These are signals your body sends to let you know that something bad might happen. If you get those signals, you should listen to them.

If you come up against a bully and feel you are in danger, get away as fast as you can. Don't stay in a place where you could get hurt. Then be sure to tell an adult you trust what happened.

For You to Do

Charlie was picking on Tyler, but Tyler was able to walk away. Make your own comic strip showing what happened. Be sure to include what each kid said.

Tyler was in the library doing his homework.

Charlie asked if he could copy Tyler's homework, and Tyler said no.

Charlie tried to grab Tyler's paper.

Tyler quickly picked up his things and walked away.

... And More to Do

If Tyler had stayed in the library, he might have let Charlie copy his homework or he might have gotten into a fight with him. When he thought about those outcomes, walking away seemed like the best thing to do.

When you are in a difficult situation, it often helps to ask yourself two questions: "What could happen?" and "Should I stay or should I go? Now look at the following situations and help these kids answer those questions.

Zack is at the supermarket with his mom. She's shopping in one aisle, and he's in another aisle when he sees Sonny steal a candy bar from a shelf. Sonny tells Zack to hide the candy bar in his pocket and give it to him at school the next day. Zack doesn't want to. Sonny calls Zack a baby and a jerk.

What could happen?

_____

_____

_____

Should Zack stay or should he go?

_____

Leslie and Ashley both live on the third floor in the same building. One day the girls get to the staircase at the same time. Ashley dares Leslie to walk down the stairs with her eyes closed. She tells Leslie, "I bet you're too scared to do that." Leslie is afraid. Then Ashley starts to cluck and says, "I can't wait to tell everyone what a chicken you are."

What could happen?

_____

_____

_____

Should Leslie stay or should she go?

_____

Morgan wanted to borrow a video game from his friend Luke. Luke had told Morgan that he wouldn't be home but that he would leave the game in the mailbox. When Morgan gets to Luke's house and starts to open the mailbox, Luke's older brother Mark says, "What do you think you're doing?" Morgan tries to explain, but Mark raises a fist and says, "Don't touch that game."

What could happen?

_____

_____

_____

Should Morgan stay or should he go?

_____

Activity 16   Tell an Adult You Trust

For You to Know

There are many times when you should tell an adult about bullying. That is especially true if you are in danger, unable to handle things yourself, afraid you'll be hurt, or afraid someone else will get hurt.

If you're frightened or feel like you are in danger, it's important to tell an adult you trust. If no one knows, no one can help you.

Owen is in the school band. Every Thursday, he carries his trumpet to school in a big case. And every Thursday, a bunch of older kids follow him to school. He's always afraid. They call him names and make fun of him as he walks by, and they try to grab his trumpet case. One time they beat him up. This Thursday, they got the case away from him. They opened it and were about to throw his trumpet in the garbage when a car happened to drive by. The boys didn't want to get caught, so they dumped the trumpet on the street and ran away. Owen was able to get his trumpet back, but he was very frightened and upset. This was something he couldn't handle himself. Finally Owen told his parents what was happening. They made sure he didn't walk to school alone.

Sometimes kids don't want to tell anyone if they are being bullied or if they know someone else could be in danger, because they're afraid the bully will find out and then the bullying will get worse. If you are afraid the bully will find out you said something, be sure to tell that to the adult you speak to. That adult can be sure not to mention your name or say who reported the bullying.

For You to Do

Telling his parents helped Owen. Here are some of the people kids usually turn to for help. Put a check next to the people you could talk to if you were being bullied and couldn't handle it by yourself, or if you knew that someone else needed help.

Except for your parents, write the name of the person. Are there other people you would add to the list?

_____ Your parents

_____ Your older sister or brother _____

_____ Another relative _____

_____ A teacher _____

_____ A guidance counselor _____

_____ A coach _____

_____ A doctor or nurse _____

_____ A neighbor _____

_____ A religious leader _____

Others: _____

_____

_____

Remember, if you are being bullied and need help, you don't have to handle it by yourself. There are people you can talk to.

... *And More to Do*

Do you agree or disagree with these statements?

You should tell an adult if you are being bullied and you are afraid.

_____ Agree   _____ Disagree

You should tell an adult if you are being bullied and you can't handle it yourself.

_____ Agree   _____ Disagree

You should tell an adult if a friend is being bullied and is afraid or in danger.

_____ Agree   _____ Disagree

You should tell an adult if you know that a bully is going to hurt someone, even if the person isn't a friend.

_____ Agree   _____ Disagree

Telling an adult about bullying is sometimes the best and safest thing to do.

_____ Agree   _____ Disagree

No one has to put up with bullying.

_____ Agree   _____ Disagree

If you checked "Agree" for all of these statements, then you've learned a lot about dealing with bullies!

For You to Know

Sometimes you can handle bullying by yourself. But sometimes bullying involves dangerous situations where you or someone else could get hurt. If that happens, you should always tell an adult you trust. That's telling, not tattling.

Telling and tattling are very different. Tattletales talk in order to get the person they're talking about in trouble. Very often, what they tattle about is none of their business.

Like Sonia: *She saw her sister use their mother's makeup, something her sister knows she's not allowed to do. So Sonia told their mother. Sonia did that only to get her sister in trouble.*

That's tattling.

Telling is not meant to get anyone is trouble. The purpose of telling is to report a dangerous situation and to protect yourself or someone else from getting hurt.

Like Chris: *He and a bunch of kids were at the town swimming pool when he saw Colin push Megan under the water and hold her there. Then he saw Colin do the same thing to two other kids. So he told the lifeguard what he saw.*

That's telling about a dangerous situation.

For You to Do

Read these situations and decide whether you think the person is telling or tattling.

Wednesday is library day in Ms. Scofield's class. Carla was supposed to return her library book, but she forgot it. Before it was time for the class to go to the library, Andrew told Ms. Scofield that Carla forgot to bring in her book.

Is Andrew telling or tattling? _____

Why do you think that?

_____

_____

_____

_____

Greg brought his library book with him. But before he got to the classroom, Chester and Jack pushed him into the boys' bathroom, took his backpack, and threw it into the toilet. The boys told Greg that if he told what they did, he'd be sorry. When he got to the classroom, Ms. Scofield asked Greg why his backpack was wet. Greg was afraid of Chester and Jack, but he was also tired of being bullied. So when they were alone, he told Ms. Scofield what happened.

Is Greg telling or tattling? _____

Why do you think that?

_____

_____

_____

_____

Serena and Tanya are good friends. Tanya knows that Serena is having a hard time with a few kids at her bus stop. They pick on her and make fun of her every day. By the time Serena gets to school, she is miserable. For the past few days, Serena has been absent. She says she doesn't feel well, but Tanya knows that she's afraid of the kids on the bus. Serena hasn't told her parents what's happening. So Tanya decides to tell her mother about the bullying, and her mother calls Serena's parents.

Is Tanya telling or tattling? _____

Why do you think that?

_____

_____

_____

_____

... And More to Do

Sometimes it can be hard to decide if you should tell anyone about a situation you see, because it isn't always clear whether it would be telling or tattling. Read each of these and then say if you would tell or not, and why. If you aren't sure, talk it over with a friend or family member.

You overhear a kid say to your friend, "If you don't give me that sweatshirt, I'll beat you up." Later that day, your friend has a black eye and his sweatshirt is missing.

_____ I would tell   _____ I wouldn't tell

because _____

_____.

You overhear a kid teasing your friend for getting the best grade in the class on a math test.

_____ I would tell   _____ I wouldn't tell

because _____

_____.

You see a kid brush your friend's glasses onto the floor and step on them.

_____ I would tell   _____ I wouldn't tell

because _____

_____.

You see two kids pushing your friend around on the playground.

_____ I would tell   _____ I wouldn't tell

because _____

_____.

For You to Know

There are many different strategies you can try when you come up against a bully. Not all of them will work every time or in every situation, and you may have to try more than one. When you're thinking about which strategy to try, it can help to use problem-solving skills. That will let you look at the situation from different points of view so you can find the best solution.

Nate and Molly live next door to each other. Nate always picks on Molly. He calls her names and makes fun of everything she does: the way she runs, the way she throws a ball, her sneakers—everything! That makes Molly angry. One day, she got so angry that she yelled at Nate and called him names back. But that just made Nate laugh and pick on Molly even more. Molly realized that she had to find a solution, so she decided try the problem-solving steps she had learned about in school:

1. Describe your problem.

   That was easy for Molly. Her problem was that Nate was constantly teasing her.

2. Ask for help if you need it. You can ask a friend, a sister or brother, a parent, or anyone else who might be able to help. Don't think you have to do this on your own.

   Molly decided to talk with her cousin Aaron because he was older and always had good ideas.

3. Think of all the possible solutions and evaluate them. Which ones are doable? Which ones are reasonable? Which ones can you pull off?

   They made a list and evaluated each possible solution. Molly could:

   - *avoid Nate. That would be hard because they live next door to each other.*

   - *stick with a friend. That would work some of the time, when Molly had friends over to play, but not all the time.*

- *ignore Nate. That might work.*

- *tell Nate how she feels. That might be something to try.*

- *make a joke. Molly wasn't very good at that so she didn't think she could pull it off.*

- *walk away. Molly was pretty sure that Nate would just follow her.*

- *tell an adult. Molly wasn't afraid of Nate, so she didn't think she had to tell anyone besides her cousin.*

4. Choose one strategy and try it.

   Molly decided that the best thing to do was to tell Nate how she feels. So she said, "I feel sad and angry when you make fun of me, and I want you to stop." But Nate didn't stop.

5. If it doesn't work, try something else.

   Molly decided to ignore Nate. She pretended that she didn't hear anything he said. No matter what Nate did, Molly acted like she didn't even notice. Pretty soon Nate gave up. Picking on Molly wasn't fun anymore.

For You to Do

Think of a problem you have with a bully. See if you can help solve it by using the problem-solving steps.

1. Describe the problem.

    _____

    _____

2. Ask for help if you need it. Who could you ask?

    _____

    _____

3. Think of all the strategies you've learned about. Write down your possible solutions and how well you think they would work.

    _____

    _____

    _____

    _____

4. Which strategy do you think you should try first? Tell why.

    _____

    _____

    _____

5. If it doesn't work, what do you think you should try next? Tell why.

_____

_____

_____

... *And More to Do*

See if you can help these kids. Put a check next to the strategies you think might work. Then put a star next to the strategy each should try first.

Danny signed up for the afterschool soccer team. On the first day, he's in the locker room when Mike, an older boy on the team, starts to tease him. He calls Danny "Shorty" and "Newbie" and other names. Then he grabs Danny's soccer shirt from his locker and holds it up high so that Danny can't reach it. Finally Mike tosses the shirt to Danny and says, "Welcome to the team. Now you know who's boss."

What do you think Danny should do?

☐ Avoid Mike.   ☐ Make a joke.

☐ Stick with a friend.   ☐ Walk away.

☐ Ignore Mike.   ☐ Tell an adult.

☐ Tell Mike how he feels.

Lee Ann is reading when her older brother Brad comes into her room and starts picking on her. First he tells her that her new haircut looks terrible. "Get out of here," Lee Ann shouts. Then he calls her names because she reads all the time. "Leave me alone," she yells. Then he makes fun of the posters she has over her bed. Lee Ann explodes. "I hate you," she screams. Brad just laughs at her.

What do you think Lee Ann should do?

☐ Avoid Brad.   ☐ Make a joke.

☐ Stick with a friend.   ☐ Walk away.

☐ Ignore Brad.   ☐ Tell an adult.

☐ Tell Brad how she feels.

Help for Kids to Stand Up to and Deal with Bullies

When Carlos gets on the school bus in the morning, a group of kids always tease him because he stutters. They call him names and imitate the way he talks. One day, a girl who is a friend of the bullies gets on at the next stop, and she sits in the seat next to Carlos. She pretends to talk to him, but she is actually just imitating him. The other kids start to laugh.

What do you think Carlos should do?

- ☐ Avoid these kids.
- ☐ Stick with a friend.
- ☐ Ignore these kids.
- ☐ Tell these kids how he feels.

- ☐ Make a joke.
- ☐ Walk away.
- ☐ Tell an adult.

Playful Teasing or Bullying?

For You to Know

Everybody gets teased at one time or another. Some teasing is just playful. It isn't meant to be hurtful. But some teasing can be mean. That kind of teasing is bullying.

Did anyone ever tease you in a playful way? Maybe your aunt said how cute your new haircut is and called you a supermodel. Or your neighbor said how much you've grown and asked when you're going to try out for the NBA. You know they aren't trying to make you feel bad. They're just being playful.

If you don't like that type of teasing, the first thing you should do is say something like: "Please don't tease me that way. I don't like it." Don't yell or shout. Be polite. It's likely that the person doing the teasing never even realized you were upset and will stop once you say something. Of course, you might feel funny speaking that way to a grown-up, like your neighbor or your aunt. In that case, you can ask your parents or another adult to say something for you.

Sometimes teasing can turn mean and hurtful. For example, suppose someone knows you hate your new haircut and keeps making fun of it or someone knows you feel uncomfortable about how tall you are and keeps pointing it out. That isn't playful teasing—it's bullying. One of the best things you can try is to ignore it. After all, what's the fun of bothering someone who doesn't get bothered!

Other things you can try are walking away or talking to the bully and saying how you feel or making a joke. And of course, avoid the bully if you can.

Just be sure not to bully back and try not to let your feelings show.

For You to Do

Think of a time when someone teased you in a playful way without meaning to hurt your feelings. Tell what happened.

_____

_____

_____

Did the teasing bother you, even though the person didn't mean it to?

_____

Did you say anything to the person? If so, what did you say?

_____

If you didn't say anything, think of something you could have said. Write it here.

_____

Did you ask your parents or another adult to say something for you? If not, will you do that if the same thing happens again?

_____

... And More to Do

Now think of a time when someone teased you to be mean and hurtful. What happened?

_____

_____

_____

How did you react?

_____

_____

Did the teasing stop?

_____

What could you do the next time?

_____

_____

_____

_____

_____

For You to Know

People react differently to nicknames. A nickname that one person thinks is okay, and might even like, could be a name that another person wouldn't like at all. It's up to the person being called the nickname to say whether it's okay or not.

A nickname is a name that is used in place of a person's real name. Calling someone by a nickname the person likes is fine. But calling someone by a nickname that person doesn't like is name-calling.

Sometimes kids give another kid a nickname because they think it's funny. They really don't mean to be hurtful. If someone gives you a nickname you don't like, it's up to you to say so. Don't expect others to be able to read your mind. Stand up for yourself and say, "Please don't call me that." Many times that will work.

Of course there are other things you can try, like these kids did:

Kevin called Billy "Jingle-Jangle" because Billy's last name rhymed with "jangle." Kevin thought it was funny, but Billy didn't like the name. So when Kevin called him that, Billy just ignored it. It took a little while, but finally Kevin stopped.

Here's what James did. Karen called James "Einstein" because he was such a good student. James didn't like the name, so he made a joke about it. He told Karen that if she studied really hard and got better grades, he'd let her be his assistant. Karen laughed. She thought it was funny. And soon she stopped calling him the nickname he didn't like.

Some people have nicknames that they like being called by one person, but not by others.

Like Jen: Jen's family calls her "Miss Kitty" because she likes cats so much. Jen likes that, but she doesn't like when other people do it. So when Tony called her "Miss Kitty" in class, she said, "I feel silly when you call me 'Miss Kitty.' I want you to stop, please." Tony didn't realize that he was bothering Jen, and he stopped using the nickname.

For You to Do

Do you have a nickname? What is it? _____

Is it a name you like? _____

Do you have a nickname that only certain people in your family use? _____

What is it? _____

Do you mind if other people use your family nickname? _____

If people call you a name that you do not like, what do you do?

_____

Did you ever ask someone to stop calling you a certain name? _____

What did you say? _____

_____

Did that work? _____

What else could you do?

_____

_____

_____

... And More to Do

Read these situations, and decide whether each involves name-calling or a nickname. If it's name-calling, tell what you think the person being called the name could do.

Jeremy has very curly hair. Eric has started to call Jeremy "Curly." Jeremy doesn't like it. He asked Eric to stop, but Eric wouldn't. So Jeremy asked him again. Eric still calls him "Curly."

Is it a nickname or name-calling? If it's name-calling, what could Jeremy do?

_____

_____

Ellie is shorter than her friend who is also named Ellie. The kids call her "Little Ellie" and call the other girl "Big Ellie." Both Ellies think it's a good way to tell each other apart.

Is it a nickname or name-calling? If it's name-calling, what could Ellie do?

_____

_____

Melinda has bright red hair. Her mother and father call her "Scarlet" sometimes. Her best friend, Lola, heard them use that name, so she started using it too. Being called "Scarlet" by someone outside her family made Melinda feel funny. But since Lola was her best friend, she said it would be okay for Lola to call her that when other kids weren't around. So now Lola calls her "Scarlet" only when they are alone.

Is it a nickname or name-calling? If it's name-calling, what could Melinda do?

_____

_____

David just got glasses. His sister Rebecca has started calling him "Bug Eyes," a name he doesn't like. He asked her to stop, but she wouldn't. So he started calling her "Big Foot" because she has very large feet.

Is Rebecca using a nickname or name-calling? If it's name-calling, what could David do?

_____

_____

Is David using a nickname or name-calling? If it's name-calling, what could Rebecca do?

_____

_____

Activity 21

Don't Put Up with Put-Downs

For You to Know

Sometimes teasing gets really bad, like when someone puts you down by imitating you or saying mean, insulting things over and over again. That kind of bullying can make you feel bad about yourself, but you can help yourself feel better.

"You're such a jerk." "You're so ugly." "You're so fat." If anyone has ever said things like that to you or imitated you in a mean way, then you know how it bad it can make you feel. And usually the kid who does that doesn't do it just once. That kind of bully does it over and over again.

So what can you do? In earlier activities, you learned about using positive self-talk to help you look and act brave and to ignore a bully. Self-talk can help you deal with put-downs as well, by focusing on the good things about you.

That's what Lilly did when Samantha kept putting her down by calling her "Lisping Lilly." Instead of thinking about her speech problem, Lilly thought about all of the things that she was good at. In her head she said, "I'm a good dancer. I'm a good friend. I'm nice to people." And that helped her ignore Samantha and her nasty remarks.

So instead of concentrating on the negative things that the bully is saying about you, try to think about the positive things about you—the things that you like about yourself—and keep saying them over and over again in your head.

Don't Pick on Me

For You to Do

Here are some examples of positive self-talk. Circle the ones you could say to yourself.

I'm smart.

I'm someone you can count on.

I'm good at games.

I'm nice to people.

I'm a good friend.

I try to do my best.

I'm a good painter.

I'm a good singer.

I'm good at math.

I keep my room clean.

I'm helpful.

I try to smile.

I take care of my things.

I'm nice to my little sister (or brother).

Now add some other things that you could say:

_____

_____

_____

... *And More to Do*

Did anyone ever say something insulting about you to your face? Or imitate you and make fun of the way you do something? Or put you down if made a mistake? Write about what happened. If this hasn't happened to you, write about someone it did happen to, or make up a story. Be sure to say how the kid being picked on felt and how using positive self-talk helped or could have helped.

_____

_____

_____

_____

_____

_____

_____

_____

_____

_____

_____

_____

_____

_____

> ### *For You to Know*
>
> Harassment is any behavior that makes you feel bad and keeps going on and on, even after you ask the person doing it to stop. No one has to put up with harassment.

You may have heard the word "harassment," especially at school. Many schools have a "No Harassment" policy.

Harassment can be irritating—like if someone keeps poking you in the arm over and over after you ask that person to stop. It may not hurt, but it's very annoying. And that's why the person does it—to annoy you!

Harassment can be embarrassing—like if someone plays a prank on you. The prank can be silly or serious.

Harassment can also be threatening—like if someone tries to touch you without your permission.

For You to Do

Brianna wants to be John's friend, so she tries to sit with him at lunch every day. She calls him after school and hangs around wherever he is. John would rather spend his time with other boys, playing basketball or video games, but Brianna keeps following him. It's not that John doesn't like Brianna; he just doesn't want to be friends with her. John is annoyed and embarrassed, especially because his friends have been teasing him about Brianna.

John has asked her to stop following him and calling him, but she hasn't stopped, so he asked his older brother for advice. His brother suggested that John talk to Brianna and tell her how he feels.

What do you think John could say? Put it in the form of an I-message. Remember to be respectful. Don't use insults or put-downs.

_____

_____

Do you think it would help if John practices what he's going to say before he speaks to Brianna? Tell why or why not.

_____

_____

Would you be able to talk to someone like John did? Tell why or why not.

_____

_____

Pretend that you are John and practice what you would say to Brianna.

... And More to Do

Harassment can bring on lots of different feelings. Complete these words by adding the missing vowels to find out what some of these feelings are.

H: H ___ R T

A: ___ N N ___ Y ___ D

R: R ___ D ___ C ___ L ___ ___ S

A: ___ N X ___ ___ ___ S

S: S ___ D

S: S C ___ R ___ D

M: M ___ S ___ R ___ B L ___

E: ___ M B ___ R ___ S S ___ D

N: N ___ R V ___ ___ S

T: T R ___ ___ B L ___ D

For You to Know

Bullies who tease, say mean things, or play embarrassing or hurtful tricks sometimes try to act as if they're only kidding. They try to make you feel even worse by saying, "Can't you take a joke?"

Some jokes that kids play on one another are funny.

Like what Ashton did to Caden: He made a fake poster by putting Caden's face on a real poster of Caden's favorite baseball player. Caden thought that was funny.

But some jokes aren't funny.

Sari didn't think it was funny when Rose put her face on a picture of a giant balloon and labeled it "Tubby."

Bullies like Rose often try to make you feel like there's something wrong with you if you don't get the joke. That can make the bullying hurt even more. But why should you get the joke when there's nothing funny about what's happening?

- Being teased about something that bothers you isn't funny.

- Being made fun of isn't funny.

- Being called a name you don't like isn't funny.

- Having a mean prank played on you isn't funny.

So what can you do? When a bully says, "I was just kidding" or "Can't you take a joke?" don't yell. Don't shout. Don't start a fight. The first thing you should always do is to stand up for yourself by saying: "It's not a joke, and I don't think it's funny." Then walk away and try to avoid the bully as much as you can.

For You to Do

Read each of these situations and decide whether you think it's a joke or not. If it's not a joke, tell what you think the kid being picked on could do.

Ben sat down in the lunchroom, opened his lunchbox, and took out his sandwich. Then he reached for his juice box. When he picked it up, all the juice came pouring out. Someone had punched a hole in the bottom. Ben's shirt and pants were soaked. He was very upset. Then he saw Robby and Nicholas laughing. Robby said, "Can't you take a joke?"

Is it a joke or not a joke? If it's not a joke, what could Ben do?

_____

_____

At the end of the school day, Keisha put on her coat and walked to the bus with her friend Isabel. As she walked along, other kids smiled at her and said, "Happy birthday." Keisha didn't know what was going on. She started to get confused. Then Isabel told her that she had put a sign on the back of Keisha's coat, saying, "Wish me a happy birthday." Keisha was embarrassed. Isabel said, "It was just a joke."

Is it a joke or not a joke? If it's not a joke, what could Keisha do?

_____

_____

Stefan always wanted to play with his older brother Miguel and his friends, but they didn't want to include him. They thought he was a pest and decided to teach him a lesson. So one day Miguel and his friends took Stefan to the park to play hide-and-seek. They told Stefan to be "It." But when Stefan turned his back to count to ten, instead of hiding, all the older boys ran away and left Stefan alone in the park. When he couldn't find the other boys, Stefan was scared. He had never been alone in the park before. Later, Miguel teased Stefan for being afraid. "We were only kidding," he said.

Is it a joke or not a joke? If it's not a joke, what could Stefan do?

_____

_____

Help for Kids to Stand Up to and Deal with Bullies

... And More to Do

Has anyone ever played a joke on you that you thought was funny? What was it?

_____

_____

_____

Has anyone ever done something to you and said it was a joke, but you thought it wasn't funny? Write about what happened.

_____

_____

_____

Tell whether you think the person actually meant it to be funny or was really trying to bother you.

_____

_____

Tell how you felt.

_____

_____

What did you do? What else could you have done?

_____

_____

_____

For You to Know

Everybody likes to have friends and be included in what other kids do. But sometimes kids leave other kids out and make them feel like they don't belong. It's a "quiet" kind of bullying: no name-calling or teasing, no threatening, and no hitting or punching. But it can hurt just as much.

Conner knows how it feels to be left out. He likes to play baseball and he practices a lot. He really wants to play with some boys who live a few blocks away and go to a different school. Every day he goes to the park where they play, but they never ask him to join their game even though they know he wants to. They won't even give him a try.

One afternoon, Conner was sitting outside his house when his aunt came by. By this time he was really feeling down on himself. His aunt saw how sad Conner looked, so she asked what was wrong.

Conner told her about the boys who wouldn't let him play with them. "They're probably right," he said. "Why would they want to play with me? I'm not as tall as they are and I probably wouldn't be able to keep up with them."

His aunt was surprised. "Conner, you're a very good baseball player. Don't let those boys convince you that you're not. And don't be so hard on yourself. You're saying all of these negative things. Instead, think about everything you're good at."

"Well," Conner said, "I know I'm a pretty good hitter. And I can throw a ball really far."

"That's right," his aunt said. "Those are things you're good at. Don't let those boys make you feel bad about yourself."

For You to Do

Once Conner thought about all of the good things he could do, he felt much better about himself. What do you think Conner did next? Put a check next to your answer.

☐ He decided to give up baseball and play a different sport.

☐ He went to the park and got into a fight with the kids who wouldn't let him play.

☐ He went to the park where his own friends were playing and joined their game.

That night when Conner got home, he wrote about his day in his journal. What would you write if you were Conner?

_____

_____

_____

_____

_____

_____

_____

_____

_____

_____

... *And More to Do*

Instead of focusing on negative thoughts about himself, Conner decided to think of everything he did well, and that made him feel much better about himself. What are some things that you do well? Are you good at drawing? Playing an instrument? Math? Soccer? Taking care of a pet? Singing? Helping out at home?

Give yourself a trophy for every good thing you do.

This trophy is awarded to

_____

for

_____

This trophy is awarded to

_____

for

_____

This trophy is awarded to

_____

for

_____

This trophy is awarded to

_____

for

_____

For You to Know

One of the meanest forms of bullying is the silent treatment. That's when a bully won't talk to you and acts as if you aren't even there.

Stacey was having a problem with her friend Kristen. So she sent an e-mail to Dr. Advice, the host of a website called "Helping Kids." Here's what she wrote:

```
Dear Dr. Advice,

For the last few weeks, my friend Kristen has been acting weird. She
and I have been friends forever. The problems started when Kristen
joined the swim team. First she wouldn't wait for me so we could walk
home from school together. Then she started having lunch with the
girls on the swim team and not asking me to sit with them. Then she
wouldn't return my text messages or phone calls. Now she walks by me
in the hall like I'm not even there. She totally ignores me. It hurts
a lot and makes me feel awful. My older sister says I should just
forget about it. She says I should stick with my other friends. What
do you think?

Stacey
```

Dr. Advice wrote back to Stacey:

```
Dear Stacey,

I call this kind of behavior the "silent treatment," and it's a very
mean kind of bullying. I think your sister has given you good advice;
you might also try to make some new friends. Another great way to
help yourself is to make a list of all of the qualities that make you
who you are--not the things that you are good at, but the qualities
that are on the inside. The list will help you remember what is
special about you. I'll send you a list to give you some ideas.

Dr. Advice
```

For You to Do

Here is the list of qualities that Dr. Advice sent Stacey. Circle the ones that you think apply to you.

Friendly	Responsible	Respectful
Helpful	Generous	Kind
Loyal	Honest	A good listener
Dependable	Considerate	Trustworthy

What would you add to this list?

_____ _____ _____

_____ _____ _____

_____ _____ _____

... *And More to Do*

Stacey's sister suggested that she stick with her other friends. Dr. Advice thought that was a good idea and also suggested that she could try to make some new friends. Think about the friends you already have, the ones who treat you well and make you feel good about yourself.

What do you have in common with these friends?

_____

_____

Tell why you like spending time with them.

_____

_____

How did you meet them?

_____

_____

One easy way to meet a new friend is through interests you both share, like basketball or music. What are your favorite activities?

_____

_____

What could you say to be friendly to another kid at that activity?

_____

_____

Don't Pick on Me

For You to Know

Threatening words can be very scary. If a bully threatens you or someone else, and you're afraid of what might happen, tell an adult you trust—especially if the bully is older or bigger than you or the other kid. And if you are afraid that the bully will find out you told, be sure to tell the adult you speak to that you do not want the bully to know it was you who reported the threat.

Chelsea was at the movies and she went to the bathroom. No one was there except for two girls she knew from school. They were smoking and they told Chelsea that she better not tell anyone about it. When she went back to her seat, Chelsea didn't say anything to her friends about what had happened. She thought that would be tattling.

The next day, Chelsea saw the two girls at school. They came up very close to her and told her again that she'd better not say anything or she'd be sorry. Chelsea didn't know what they might do, but she felt like they were threatening her and that made her nervous.

That night, Chelsea talked to her brother. Together, they decided that the best thing for her to do was to stick with her friends. So Chelsea made sure that she sat with her friends on the bus and in the lunchroom and on the playground. Having her friends around her made Chelsea feel much safer. And soon the two girls left Chelsea alone.

For You to Do

Isaiah is in line in the school cafeteria when Carl comes up behind him and says in a low, mean voice, "Give me your lunch money—or else!" Isaiah is frightened and hands his money over. Then Carl warns Isaiah that he better not tell anyone what happened or he'll be sorry. This isn't the first time Carl has stolen Isaiah's money and threatened him.

How would you feel if you were Isaiah?

_____

Would you give Carl your lunch money? Why or why not?

_____

_____

What do you think would happen if Isaiah made sure he that he was with a friend at lunchtime?

_____

_____

What do you think would happen if Isaiah just walked away from Carl?

_____

_____

If you were Isaiah, would you tell anyone what had happened? Why or why not?

_____

_____

... And More to Do

Being threatened can bring on all kinds of feelings. It can make you nervous, jumpy, anxious, fearful, or frightened. It can make your heart race and can make you breathe very fast. But if you let a bully know that's how you're feeling, the bullying might get worse. Remember, that's what the bully wants. So it's important to try to calm down and not let the bully see how you feel.

Deep breathing is one way to help yourself calm down and feel less nervous. It takes some practice to be able to do that, so try this and see how it works:

- Sit in a comfortable chair. Close your eyes and breathe in and out. Concentrate on your breathing.

- Then take a deep breath and let it out very slo-o-o-wly. Do this three times. Let your breath out as slowly as you can.

- Now count to five before you take your next breath. That will make your breathing even slower. Repeat this four more times.

- By now you should be more relaxed and calmer. Before you get up from the chair, breathe regularly for a minute or two.

Practice breathing deeply for a while until you are comfortable with it. Then, if someone threatens you or tries to frighten you, you'll be able to calm down. You'll be in control of your feelings. And you won't give the bully the satisfaction of knowing that you're afraid.

For You to Know

Some bullies don't use words. Instead, they push, shove, punch, hit or do other things that can hurt you. Sometimes they take and destroy your property. These bullies can be especially scary. If someone tries to hurt you or takes and destroys your property, first try to get away to a place where you'll be safe. Then be sure to tell an adult you trust.

Ethan had just gotten a new video game for his birthday. He was so excited that he couldn't wait to show it to all his friends. On the bus to school, Ethan and his friends talked about the game and made plans to meet later on and play it. Roger listened to them talking. Roger was two grades ahead of Ethan and he had a reputation as a bully who often tried to hurt other kids.

When Ethan got off the bus, he headed to the library to return an overdue book. Roger followed him. He grabbed Ethan and pushed him into a place where no one could see them. Then he knocked Ethan down, took his backpack, and stole the new video game. As soon as Roger was out of sight, Ethan ran into the school so he wouldn't be alone if Roger came back.

Then he went to see the school nurse. He said he didn't feel well and that he wanted to go home. The nurse noticed a bump on Ethan's head and asked how it had happened. At first Ethan didn't say anything. But the nurse could tell that something was really bothering him, so she asked what was wrong. That was when Ethan decided to tell her what Roger had done.

For You to Do

Ethan didn't try to fight back and he didn't try to keep Roger from stealing his game.

Do you think Ethan was smart to not fight back? Why or why not?

_____

_____

_____

Do you think Ethan should have tried to keep Roger from getting his game? Why or why not?

_____

_____

_____

Why was it so important for Ethan to get away from Roger and to a place where he would be safe?

_____

_____

_____

Would you have told the nurse what happened? Why or why not?

_____

_____

_____

... *And More to Do*

Has a bully ever used physical force on you, like punching or hitting or shoving you? If it didn't happen to you, then you may have seen it happen to someone else, and that can also be very scary. Write about what happened.

_____

_____

_____

Were you able to get away?

_____

If you were able to get away, how did you do it?

_____

_____

Did you tell anyone what happened?

_____

If you did, who did you tell?

_____

For You to Know

Gossip is when people spread stories that aren't any of their business or talk about someone behind that person's back in a mean way. A rumor is a story that is repeated without anyone being sure it is true. Kids who spread rumors and gossip just to be mean and hurtful are bullies.

If anyone ever gossiped about you, then you probably know how hurtful it can be. And it really doesn't matter if the story is true or not. Even a true story might be something you don't want other kids to know and talk about. It's none of their business.

Michael's parents are getting a divorce. Kids in his class were talking about it to each other. That made Michael very upset.

Jenna is going to start special classes to help her with her learning disability. She saw some kids whispering and pointing at her. When she got closer to them, they stopped talking. That made her feel uncomfortable.

A rumor is a story that is spread without anyone being sure it is true. Very often, a rumor is meant to hurt the person the story is about.

Alex and Jorge are on the same soccer team. Alex doesn't like Jorge, so he told the other kids on the team that the only reason Jorge made the team is because the coach is Jorge's father's best friend. He said no other team wanted Jorge. Soon all the kids were talking about Jorge behind his back and calling him names. He felt terrible. He didn't even want to play soccer anymore.

For You to Do

How would you feel if you were Michael? Would it bother you that kids were talking about your family?

_____

_____

How would you feel if you were Jenna? Would it bother you that kids were talking about you behind you back and not to your face?

_____

_____

How would you feel if you were Jorge?

_____

_____

Did anyone ever gossip or spread a rumor about you? What was it? How did it make you feel?

_____

_____

Did you ever gossip or spread a rumor about someone else? Did you think of what you were doing as bullying?

_____

_____

Don't Pick on Me

... *And More to Do*

No one has to put up with gossip and rumors. Here are some thing you can do to stop this kind of bullying.

If the story is about you:

- and if the story isn't true, make sure you let people know. Ask your friends to help you out in doing this.

- and if the story is true but you don't want other kids to repeat it, let people know that too.

- and if you know who started the rumor or gossip and you feel safe, talk to that person. Remember to do it out in the open. And bring a friend along. That will probably make you feel better.

- and if you can't handle it yourself and you need help, talk to someone about it, like a brother or sister or an adult you trust.

If the story is about someone else:

- don't repeat the story;

- tell the person who told you the rumor or gossip not to repeat it either;

- if you want to help the person the story is about, try to find out what that person would like you to do. If the story isn't true, you can help to set the record straight. If the story is hurtful, you can ask others not to repeat it.

Activity 29

Telephone: It's Not Just a Game

For You to Know

Rumors and gossip spread when one person tells the story to another person, and then that person tells someone else. And it keeps going on. Soon the rumor and gossip is all over the place—and it probably isn't even the same story.

Did you ever play the game Telephone? That's when one person makes up a story and whispers it to another person. Then that person whispers it to the next person and so on. The story keeps being repeated until the last person playing the game tells the story out loud. The funny part of the game is how different that story is from the story the first person told.

That's what happens with rumors and gossip. One person tells another person who tells another person who tells … well, you get the idea. And each time the story is repeated it can change. Soon no one knows what is true and what isn't.

That's why it's so important to set the record straight. If the rumor or gossip is about you, be sure to let people know how you feel. If the story isn't true, get the facts out. If the story upsets you, let them know that too.

And if the story is about someone else, don't repeat it. That way, you won't spread false or hurtful stories.

For You to Do

Cody missed a lot of school this year because he was sick. He was going to summer school to catch up so he could start school in the fall with his regular class. A lot of the kids in his grade were gossiping about Cody. He didn't like the idea of kids talking about him behind his back, but he didn't do anything to stop the gossip. He just hoped it would go away. Then rumors started flying around. One rumor was that Cody was going to be held back. Another rumor said that he would have to go to a different school.

What do you think Cody should do? Circle the strategies that you think will help him.

Get into a fight with one of the kids who is spreading the gossip.

Ask one of the kids who is gossiping to stop.

Tell a friend how he feels.

Tell the other kids the facts.

Ask a friend to tell other kids how he feels.

Start a rumor about someone else.

Talk to his brother about how he feels.

Say nothing.

Stay home from school.

Pretend that the rumors and gossip don't bother him.

Help for Kids to Stand Up to and Deal with Bullies

... And More to Do

Madison went to the doctor for a check-up. She and her father were in the waiting room when they saw Nick come out of the doctor's office. Madison heard the doctor say to Nick's mother, "He should be better soon. Just be sure to keep him away from bees. That could be very, very dangerous."

When Madison got home, she called her friend Anna and told her what she had heard. At school the next day, Anna told Richie and Laila what Madison had told her. But Richie and Laila thought Anna said "boys," not "bees," and that's what they told Jim and Ahmad: that it would be very dangerous for Nick to be with other boys. Soon the boys were acting very weird when Nick was around. They wouldn't sit next to him on the bus or even play with him.

What do you think happened next? Write an ending for this story. Be sure to say how you think Nick felt and what you think he should do to set the record straight and stop the rumor.

_____

_____

_____

_____

_____

_____

_____

_____

_____

_____

For You to Know

Cyberbullying takes place over the Internet, on computers, cell phones, and other devices like that. Cyberbullies can be just as mean, threatening, and frightening as regular bullies—maybe more, because cyberbullies can get you anytime and anywhere. And often you don't know who they are.

Mariah was doing her homework when she got an e-mail from someone she didn't know. She didn't recognize the name, but she clicked on the message anyway. It said: "I know u told Jennifer lies about me. I'm going to get back at u. U BETTER WATCH OUT!!" The message was signed: "Out2GetU."

Mariah was very frightened and confused. She had never told Jennifer lies about anyone. She wondered who had sent the e-mail. Who would want to hurt her?

The first thing she thought to do was to delete the e-mail. But then she decided to show it to her father. He set up a block so Mariah would never get another message from Out2GetU again.

For You to Do

Tell whether any of these thing have happened to you or someone you know. If they have, write about what happened.

Has anyone ever sent a threatening e-mail to you or someone you know?

_____

_____

_____

Has anyone ever posted embarrassing pictures of you or someone you know online?

_____

_____

_____

Has anyone ever started a nasty rumor about you or someone you know and IM-ed it to the whole class?

_____

_____

_____

Has anyone ever sent you or someone you know a frightening text message?

_____

_____

_____

... And More to Do

Just like with bullying in person, there are strategies that you can use to protect yourself from cyberbullying.

- Don't open e-mail unless you know who it is from.

- Don't answer e-mail from a bully. This is just like ignoring the bully in person. If you ignore the bully, it won't be fun for her to pick on you anymore.

- Sign off. Try to stay away from your computer for a while. If a cyberbully sees that you aren't online, he may get bored and leave you alone.

- Stick with your friends. If a bully sends a nasty e-mail about you to your friends, ask them to stand up for you.

- Set the record straight. If a cyberbully is spreading a rumor about you, let people know the true story. Ask your friends to get the truth out too. Rumors sent by e-mail can spread very, very fast. So it's important to set the record straight as soon as you can.

- Don't bully back. In this case, bullying back would be to sending a mean e-mail to the cyberbully. That will just make things worse.

- Tell an adult you trust. The adult may want to block the bully from sending anything to you, or take other action, so don't delete any threatening e-mail.

Have you ever tried any of these strategies? _____

If you did, was it successful? _____

What happened?

_____

_____

Will you try one of the strategies in the future if you have to? Tell what you'll do.

_____

Help for Kids to Stand Up to and Deal with Bullies

For You to Know

To protect yourself online, pick user IDs and passwords that don't give away too much information about you.

Cyberbullies often cause trouble by pretending to be someone else.

Troy got a call from his friend Derek. Derek was so mad he was fuming. He wanted to know why Troy had said such mean things about him in a chat room. Troy said he hadn't done that and never would—Derek was his friend. The boys realized that someone had stolen Troy's user ID and password and pretended to be him.

Troy was really upset. He realized that it wasn't hard for a cyberbully to steal his information. His e-mail address and user ID were both "Troy" and his password was "813" for his birthday, August 13. And he had given out that information to lots of people. He had also written his user ID and password in his notebook and taped it in his locker, where it was easy for anyone to find.

What happened to Troy isn't that unusual. Here are some Internet safety tips that you should follow. They will help keep a cyberbully from picking on you.

- You want your friends to be able to send you e-mails, but you don't want strangers to be able to figure out who you are from your e-mail name. So pick an e-mail address that doesn't use your full name, your house address, or your telephone number.

- Pick a user ID and password for chat rooms and other sites that is different from your e-mail address and password.

- Make sure your user IDs and passwords are easy for you to remember, but don't give away too much information about you.

- Don't let anyone but your parents know your user IDs or passwords. That way no one will be able to log on to your account and read your e-mail or pretend to be you online.

For You to Do

Do you have a user ID and password for chat rooms and websites that you like to visit?

_____

Is your user ID also your e-mail address? _____

Does your user ID tell something about you? _____

How many people know your user ID and password?

_____

Do you think it would be easy for someone to steal your user ID and password?

_____

If you think a lot of people know your user ID and password, pick new ones. Use your imagination to think of something that will be easy for you to remember, but not easy for others to recognize. If you want to use numbers, don't use your birthday.

Does your e-mail address tell a lot about you?

_____

If your e-mail address is your full name, pick a new e-mail address too. But make sure it isn't the same as your new user ID. And be sure not to give your new user ID and password to anyone but your parents.

... *And More to Do*

See if you can help these kids pick a user ID and e-mail address that is easy to remember. Be sure neither one uses their real name.

Donny Jenkins has blue eyes and red hair. His favorite sport is baseball, and he plays second base on his team, the Sluggers. His favorite subject is math.

A good user ID for Donny is _____.

A good e-mail address for Donny is _____.

Emma O'Mara plays the flute in the school band. She has a twin brother who also plays in the band. Her favorite food is chocolate chip ice cream. Her favorite color is yellow.

A good user ID for Emma is _____.

A good e-mail address for Emma is _____.

Diego Hernandez likes to write stories and read them to his class. He even wrote a play that the class put on for Visitors' Day. His favorite book is **The Outsiders.** *He wants to be a writer when he grows up.*

A good user ID for Diego is _____.

A good e-mail address for Diego is _____.

Shandra Johnson loves to play soccer, and she's a really good goalie. Her favorite subject in school is social studies. She has a cat named Oscar and a canary named Buddie.

A good user ID for Shandra is _____.

A good e-mail address for Shandra is _____.

Paul Gordy is a big basketball fan. He loves the Chicago Bulls and always wears a Bulls hat and a Bulls jacket. His dream is to play professional basketball. His favorite food is pepperoni pizza.

A good user ID for Paul is _____.

A good e-mail address for Paul is _____.

For You to Know

Posting embarrassing pictures online is another kind of cyberbullying. Pictures can be sent from cell phones, posted on websites, or sent in e-mails—and it takes only a second. If a cyberbully comes after you this way, be sure to get help. Tell an adult you trust.

Darien got a call from his friend Matthew. Matthew said that all the kids in their class had gotten a message telling them to go into a chat room the kids liked. When Darien logged on, he saw that someone had posted embarrassing pictures of him. They had been taken in the locker room after gym class.

Darien thought that what happened to him must have been his fault. But it wasn't. There wasn't anything that he did wrong or anything that he could have done to prevent the cyberbully from picking on him. But that didn't stop him from getting down on himself. When he went to bed that night, he was still blaming himself for what happened.

The next day, he was so embarrassed he didn't want to go to school. When his mother asked him what was wrong, Darien didn't want to say anything. But finally he decided to tell. And that was a very good thing to do, because this was something that Darien could not handle himself. His mother got in touch with their Internet Service Provider, and they started a search to find the person who posted the pictures.

For You to Do

To help him accept that what happened wasn't his fault, Darien can think positive thoughts. Put a check next to the thoughts that will help Darien and an X next to the negative thoughts that will make him feel worse.

"This is all my fault."

"I didn't do anything to make this happen."

"I didn't do anything wrong."

"How did I let this happen?"

"They're right; I am dumb."

"I'm so stupid."

"I messed up."

"I must have done something wrong."

"This isn't my fault."

"There wasn't any way I could have stopped this."

... *And More to Do*

The pictures of Darien were posted by a cyberbully. But sometimes kids post pictures of themselves online without realizing that they might be seen by other people and used against them. These kids don't understand that you can never be certain that what you post online will remain private. So remember this: don't ever put anything online that you don't want everyone to see.

Now, imagine that you are a reporter for a newspaper. Write a short article about a girl who sent a friend a picture of herself, labeled "For Your Eyes Only." But the picture was discovered by a cyberbully. Report what happened, how the girl who sent the original picture felt, and what she did once she found out what happened.

SUNDAY NEWS

| Vol 2, No 13 | Everytown, USA | 36¢ |

Cyberbully Finds Pictures Online

Help for Kids to Stand Up to and Deal with Bullies

For You to Know

Some kids try to tell their friends what to do and how to act and who to like. You may not realize it, but kids like that are bullying their friends. Being bossy—insisting that people do things your way and like the things that you like—is a kind of bullying.

If you have a friend who is bossing you around, the first thing you should do is stand up for yourself, and let your friend know that you don't like being pushed around. Be firm, but polite. This is great time for using the I-messages that you learned about in Activity 13. Remember, an I-message states how you feel, what makes you feel that way, and what you would like the other person to do—without putting down the other person or starting a fight. It always begins with the words "I feel."

Hannah's favorite television program is "Wizard's Wonder Tales." Her best friend Alyssa says the show is stupid and calls Hannah a jerk for liking it. She also criticizes the way Hannah wears her hair and makes fun of the way Hannah dances. Hannah is beginning to feel bad about herself.

Hannah could say, "I feel hurt when you make fun of the way I look and the things I like. I don't like it when you put me down, and I want you to stop."

Joseph and Sam spend a lot of time together. They're in the same class and on the same baseball team. They also like to play video games together. But whenever Sam comes over to Joseph's house, he insists that they do what he wants. No matter what Joseph says, Sam keeps pushing to have it his way. If Joseph won't go along, Sam says he'll leave. Joseph likes having Sam as a friend, but now being with him isn't so much fun.

Joseph could say, "I feel left out because what I want to do never seems to matter. I want you to take turns with me choosing what to play."

For You to Do

Do you have a friend who is bossy? If you do, how does it make you feel?

_____

Do you think telling your friend how you feel would help?

_____

Write an I-message that you can say to your friend to stop the bullying.

_____

_____

_____

Now practice saying your I-message until you feel comfortable. That way you'll be ready the next time your friend tries to boss you around. If you use this message, write about what happens.

_____

_____

_____

... And More to Do

What are the things that you think make a good friend? Design some bumper stickers that say, "A Good Friend ..." You can choose qualities from the list below or make up your own.

- makes you feel good about yourself

- cares how you feel

- is happy when you're happy

- doesn't put you down

- helps you feel better when you are sad

- isn't bossy

- sticks up for you

- keeps a promise

- is willing to help you

- treats you with respect

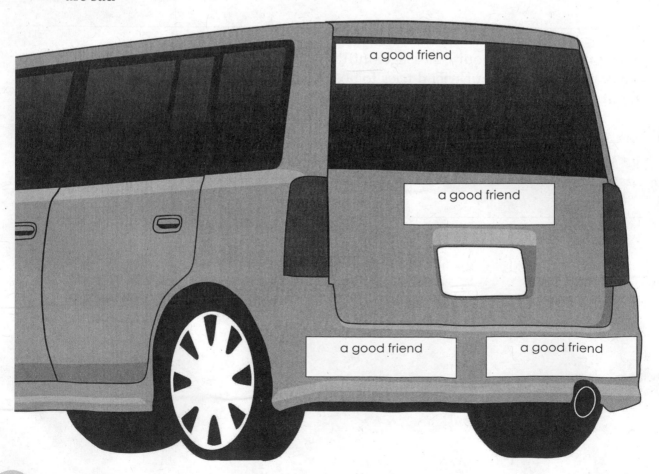

a good friend

a good friend

a good friend

a good friend

Don't Pick on Me

For You to Know

Sometimes a friend may try to talk you into doing something you don't want to do, something that you know is wrong. The friend may try to bully you into going along by making you feel guilty. If that happens, you have the right to say no.

"I'd do it for you." Did anyone ever say that to you to make you feel guilty for not caving in and doing something that you don't want to do? That's another kind of bullying that friends can do to friends.

Like Mac: *He wants Jake to keep an eye out while he takes some money from another kid's backpack. Jake knows this is wrong, and he doesn't want to go along. But Mac keeps pressuring him by saying things like: "I'd do it for you" and "I'd help you out if you needed help" and "What kind of friend are you?"*

What can Jake do? He can stand up for himself, be assertive, and say no. And he has to try to stop the conversation as soon as he can. Because the more Jake talks about not wanting to go along with Mac, the more chance Mac has to change Jake's mind.

So Jake has to say no and keep saying no. And if Mac asks him why, Jake could say, "Because I don't want to." He might give one reason, like "Because we could both get in trouble," but he shouldn't give a lot of excuses. That will only give Mac more time to talk Jake into doing what he wants.

Now here's something else to think about. If you have a friend who is always trying to talk you into doing things that you don't want to do, you should ask yourself: "Is this the kind of friend I really want?" And if the person is trying to bully you into doing something dangerous or illegal, the safest thing to do is to walk away. Very often the best thing you can do for your friend is to set an example. Your friend might just follow you.

For You to Do

Alice was trying to talk Sunny into stealing cigarettes from Sunny's grandmother's purse. Sunny didn't want to do that, and she said no. But Alice wouldn't give up. Here are a few things Sunny could do to stop the talk. After each example of what Sunny could say, add your own suggestion.

Change the subject.

If Alice says, "Let's take the cigarettes and go outside and smoke."

Sunny could say, "No. Do you think Jose is cute?"

Or she could say: _____

_____.

Make a joke.

If Alice says, "Let's take the cigarettes and go outside and smoke."

Sunny could say, "No. My grandma has her purse wired. If anyone touches it, an alarm goes off!"

Or she could say: _____

_____.

Find an alternative.

If Alice says, "Let's take the cigarettes and go outside and smoke."

Sunny could say, "No, I'm hungry. Let's get some ice cream."

Or she could say: _____

_____

... And More to Do

Look at the pictures below. For each one, write what the person being bullied could say to stop the conversation.

_____   _____

_____   _____

_____

_____

For You to Know

It's nice to have a bunch of friends to hang out with—friends who share your interests and make you feel good about yourself. But some groups of friends are different. These groups are called cliques. A clique is an exclusive group that doesn't welcome others. Usually cliques have leaders who make the rules: how to act, what to wear, and who to be friends with.

Sophia was friendly with a bunch of girls in her grade. For the most part, they liked to do the same things. But everyone in the group knew that Chloe and Marcy were the leaders. They decided who could come into the group and who would be excluded. All of the other girls went along because that was just the way it was.

Sophia never thought about what this meant until she came home from spending a few weeks in the summer with her cousin Lucy. Lucy liked to play chess, and she taught Sophia to play. It turned out that Sophia was very good at chess. When she got home she told her friends she was going to join the Chess Club at school. She was very excited about it.

But Chloe and Marcy didn't like the idea. "We don't do that," they said. They put Sophia down for wanting to play chess. And they made it clear that if she joined the Chess Club, she couldn't be in their group.

Sophia didn't know what to do. These were her friends, and now they were treating her like an outsider. Then she thought about other things the girls in the group did. They made fun of anyone who didn't "belong" and they were mean to kids they didn't like. They all followed Chloe and Marcy because they were afraid to get on their bad side.

Sophia was upset and confused, and one day, she told her grandmother about the situation. Her grandmother helped her see that the group was actually a clique, and that Chloe and Marcy were bullies. They weren't good friends and neither were the other girls who would go along with them.

So Sophia decided to join the Chess Club and make new friends: friends who didn't leave others out, friends who were nice to everyone, friends who supported her. After that, some of the other girls in the clique realized that they had been feeling the same way Sophia did. They dropped out too and they all were much happier.

For You to Do

All of the words in this word search say something about groups of friends. Find the words and circle in red the ones that apply to a clique. Circle all the other words in green.

outsider	bully	kind	nice	supportive
include	rules	mean	exclude	caring
closed	open	friendly	bossy	leader

M	C	E	X	C	L	U	D	E
T	O	U	T	S	I	D	E	R
S	C	A	R	I	N	G	K	F
U	S	R	E	K	I	N	D	R
P	O	J	S	N	I	C	E	I
P	L	E	A	D	E	R	T	E
O	K	B	N	M	R	L	O	N
R	B	B	C	E	R	R	P	D
T	U	O	T	A	X	U	E	L
I	L	S	F	N	C	L	N	Y
V	L	S	U	M	E	E	L	Y
E	Y	Y	L	U	S	S	P	D
O	M	I	N	C	L	U	D	E
U	C	L	C	L	O	S	E	D

Which words best describe your friends?

_____

_____

Don't Pick on Me

... And More to Do

Being part of a group is good for some kids, but other kids like to have just one or two friends. And there are lots of kids who are friends with more than one group. For example, they may belong to the band and play on a team, too, and be friendly with both groups.

And then there are some kids who find that their interests have changed. They might have been into soccer or gymnastics at one time and now like to do other things. They find new friends who share their new interests.

Do you like to be part of a big group of friends, or are you happier having one or two friends?

_____

What are some things that you like to do?

_____

Do your friends like to do those things too?

_____

What are some new activities that you would like to try?

_____

Do you know kids who have those interests? Could you talk to them?

_____

For You to Know

Everyone has seen bullying happen. It might be a friend who is being picked on or someone you don't know who is being teased or harassed or threatened. And seeing that can be scary—almost as scary as having it happen to you.

Have you ever seen someone being bullied? Seeing a situation like that can be very, very scary.

Patrick and Noah were on the way to baseball practice when they saw some older boys standing in a circle around Sean, a boy in their grade. One boy pushed Sean, then another one shoved him. From the look on Sean's face, Patrick and Noah could see that he was really scared.

"What do you think we should do?" Patrick asked Noah.

"I think we should just mind our own business and get out of here."

"But what about Sean?" Patrick asked. "Those guys could really hurt him."

Just doing nothing can also be upsetting. So what can you do? The first thing to know is that you should never put yourself in danger. If you see someone being bullied and you know that it isn't safe, tell an adult as soon as you can. Remember, that isn't tattling. And if you're afraid that the bully will find out you told, be sure to let the adult you talk to know that.

That's what Patrick and Noah did. As soon as they got to baseball practice, they told the coach, who went and helped Sean.

For You to Do

Not all situations are as dangerous as the one that Patrick and Noah saw, and there are things you can do when you see bullying. If you act like a friend to someone you see being teased or picked on, the bullying might stop.

Jessica knew that Eli and Darrin liked to tease Marissa. So when she saw them get in line right behind Marissa in the lunchroom, she called out to Marissa and asked her to stand with her. That way Marissa would be away from the boys.

Russell knew that some older kids on the bus sometimes picked on Justin. If the seat next to Justin was empty, one of them would sit in it and do things to annoy Justin. Otherwise they left him alone. So Russell made sure that he sat next to Justin whenever he could.

Maria knew that some mean girls would call Louisa names because she was very overweight. So she talked to Louisa and let her know that she was on her side. And she and her friends went out of their way to include Louisa and make sure that she wasn't alone.

Do you know anyone who is picked on that you could help by being a friend?

_____

What is the situation?

_____

_____

_____

_____

What could you do to help out?

_____

_____

_____

_____

How do you think that would make you feel?

_____

_____

How do you think that would make the other person feel?

_____

_____

... And More to Do

Sometimes it's not your friend who is being picked on. Sometimes it's your friend who is the bully. What can you do then? Well, first here's one thing you shouldn't do: try not to do anything that will encourage the bully, like laughing or cheering. Remember, bullies like to get attention, so any encouragement you give your friend will only make things worse for the kid being picked on.

If your friend is someone you can talk to and aren't afraid of, then try that. Maybe your friend doesn't realize that what he or she thinks is just a joke or playful teasing is really bullying. It's a good idea to ask some of your other friends to join you in talking to the bully.

But if the bullying doesn't stop, then you should ask yourself: "Is this the kind of friend I want to have?"

Do you have a friend who bullies other kids? _____

Do you think your friend realizes that you consider him or her a bully? _____

Can you talk to your friend? _____

What could you say that might help stop the bullying?

_____

_____

What could you say to get your other friends to join you?

_____

_____

Remember, don't put yourself in danger. Don't stand up to the bully yourself, if you think it's not safe. And if you think that someone might get hurt, ask an adult you trust for help.

For You to Know

Bullying is a big cause of stress for a lot of kids. Having a healthy lifestyle is one of the best ways to deal with that stress. A healthy lifestyle means eating well, exercising, and getting the right amount of sleep.

Stress is what you feel when you are worried or frightened or uncomfortable about a situation. And being attacked by a bully is certainly cause for stress.

Someone at school decided to start a campaign against Charlotte. Whoever it was spread rumors that Charlotte had stolen money from other kids' lockers and had cheated in school. The bully even posted mean remarks about her on the Internet, making fun of the way Charlotte sang and the pictures that she drew in art class and the way she dressed and wore her hair. Charlotte was miserable. She felt like she was under attack all the time.

Rather than holding in her feelings, Charlotte talked to her mother and her older sister, who helped her feel much better. Her friends gave her support and let other kids know that the rumors weren't true. She also spent time doing things she enjoys, like listening to music, writing in her journal, and reading. One very important thing Charlotte read about was how a healthy lifestyle helps people deal with stress.

Having a healthy lifestyle means:

- eating a balanced diet, with a healthy breakfast to help you start the day off right

- exercising between thirty and sixty minutes a day

- getting enough sleep; for kids your age, that means about ten hours a night

For You to Do

To find out what foods you should be eating and the correct amounts, go to mypyramid.gov, where you can make a food plan just for you. That way you'll be sure to get a variety of foods and plenty of fruits and vegetables.

Make copies of this chart and use it to keep track of your exercise and sleep, as well as to record what you ate for breakfast. Keep a record for four weeks, and see if you can improve little by little each week.

	Minutes of Exercise	**Hours of Sleep**	**Breakfast**
Sunday			
Monday			
Tuesday			
Wednesday			
Thursday			
Friday			
Saturday			

If you need to improve, set a goal to do that. Write it here:

_____

_____

...And More to Do

Spending time on activities she enjoyed helped Charlotte relax, and it can help you too.

In the space below, create a collage that shows things you like to do. If you prefer, you can use the space to draw a picture of your favorite activity or activities.

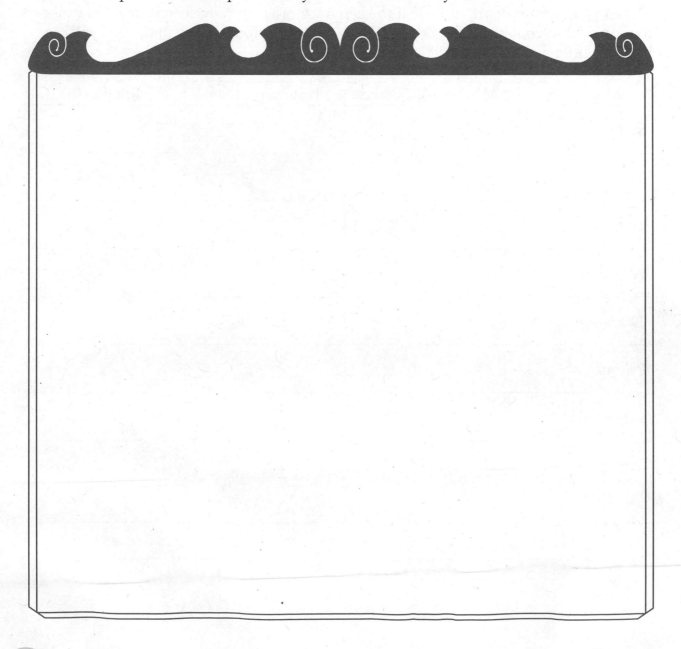

Susan Eikov Green is a writer and producer of over 150 award-winning educational programs for youth that cover such topics as bullying, character education, and drug prevention. She lives in Sherman, CT.

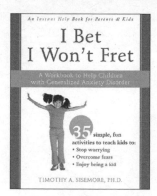

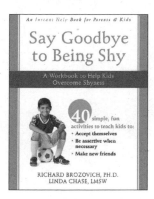
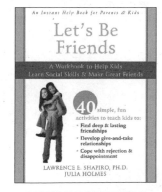